# HotWired Style

# HOT WIRED STYLE

## Principles For Building Smart Web Sites

## JEFFREY VEEN

WIRED

**WIRED**

Wired Books, Inc.
520 Third Street, Fourth Floor
San Francisco, CA 94107

Wired Books are distributed to the trade
in the United States and Canada by
Publishers Group West and in the United
Kingdom and internationally by Penguin.

First Edition 1997
Printed in the United States of America
10 9 8 7 6 5 4 3 2 1

Library of Congress Cataloging-in-Publication Data
Veen, Jeffrey.
Hotwired style : principles for building smart Web sites / Jeffrey Veen.
p.    cm.
Includes index.
ISBN 1-888869-09-7
1. Web sites – Design.          I. Title.
TK5105.888.V44 1997
025.04 – dc21                          97-30675
                                                        CIP

# Dedication

For Leslie
my partner, best friend, and beta tester

# Contents

# Acknowledgments

I came to HotWired before it was. We were a small team, we sat on the floor with PowerBooks and followed a vision to create a new medium.

That vision was made real by HotWired's creative director, Barbara Kuhr. Her endless pursuit of the principles in *HotWired Style* not only have defined the aesthetic of Web design, but have taught us all that simplicity is hard, good design is not decoration, and drop shadows are the root of all evil. I am forever grateful for her guidance and perspective.

Achieving our goals would not have been possible without the tremendous work done by the creative forces behind *Wired* magazine and Wired Digital. What an honor it is to work with amazing minds like Louis Rossetto, Kevin Kelly, John Plunkett, David Weir, Andrew Anker, Beth Vanderslice, and Gary Wolf.

I am continually awed by my coworkers and colleagues. I wish I could thank every brilliant individual who has contributed in some way to this incredible experiment we call HotWired. Specifically, I would be lost without the Interface Group: Mike Kuniavsky, Taylor, Anna McMillan, Eric Eaton, Mary Spicer, and Patrick Corcoran. Thanks also to the amazingly talented Design Group: Jonathan Louie, Erik Adigard, Sabine Messner, Jim Frew, Brady Clark, Doug Bowman, Judd

Vetrone, and Lilla Manguy. And to my colleagues who have kept HotWired (and me) going through the years: Joel Truher, jillo, Luke Knowland, Todd Elliott, Pamela Statz, Sven Heinicke, Zach Waller, Paul Boutin, Ed Anuff, June Cohen, Chip Bayers, Mark Durham, Sean Welch, Kristin Windbigler, John Alderman, Steve Silberman, Dave Winer, Derek Powazak, Thomas Reardon, David Peters, Carl Steadman, and Joey Anuff.

I never would have finished this book, nor would it be what it is, had it not been for my editor, Cate Corcoran. She forced me to think clearly, to write well, and to ship on time. I must also acknowledge everyone at Wired Books: Connie Hale, who put me on the right track and kept me there, Peter Rutten, Susanna Dulkinys, Juliette Robbins, Donna Linden, and Rosemary Sheffield.

Finally, thanks to The Geeks (mjr, kosts, bolhuijo, mitchn, planting, and nickh) and, of course, my family. What would I do without you?

Jeffrey Veen

# Foreword

It's easy to forget how young the Web is. It's hard to separate the potential from the hype. And it is nearly impossible, after hearing about this "amazing, new, transformative medium," not to be disappointed when you visit a Web site. If this is The Future, why is it so slow, dumb, and ugly?

At HotWired, we've been wrestling with this question for nearly three years now, and although we still have more questions than answers, here are a few things we believe are true:

First, when you see *slow, dumb, and ugly*, think *real-time, sound, and motion*, for that is where the medium is headed. Even now, as the Web develops from HTML to DHTML, Web designers are working more as interactive film-makers than as graphic designers.

Second, remember that it took about thirty years for the horseless carriage to become a car. Our current discussions of Web pages are on the same level as carriage lamps and running boards. We still aren't working on the car, but we're building the infrastructure and figuring out the rules. The next generation – the kids who are growing up in a world that has always had the Web, the 13 year olds building JavaScript interfaces – these are the people who will figure out how to truly engage the medium.

Third and most important, there are no experts. If someone tells you they are a Web expert, don't believe them.
There are only smart, enthusiastic, curious collaborators. The
principles Jeff writes about in this book simply can't be
achieved without a lot of intense, messy collaboration
between editors, designers, and engineers. If you don't like
working this way, you won't enjoy building Web sites.

We have been lucky enough to work with some great
collaborators, from the first tiny team of fourteen in the
summer of 1994 to the current group of nearly 100. Jeff has
been with us from the beginning, and he's one of the best
there is. May you be so lucky.

Barbara Kuhr
Creative Director, Wired Ventures

# Embrace
# the Medium

Say this out loud: The Web is not print. The Web is not television. The Web is not a CD-ROM.

Seem obvious? It's not. Say it again. Although it has words like books, images like TV, and multimedia like CD-ROMs, the Web is singular. It has its own language, aesthetic, issues, and problems and yet represents a convergence of nearly all other media. Its content must be built to travel across vast networks to unknown devices and browsers.

But don't throw out everything you know about working in other media. Not yet. Making great Web sites forces you to take classic design principles and apply them in ways you'd never dream of if you were designing a poster or making a movie.

The Web relies on the divine design commandment that form follows function – and the age-old battle between form and function is waged at every stage of Web design. There is a constant pull between art and utility, extravagance and practicality, entertainment and reference. Online publishing is both a craft and a science – and Web sites range from deep databases to multimedia experiences.

## The library and the gallery

Spend an hour surfing the Web. Jump from site to site. Be random. Ignore the specific content and just look at the Web sites as they come and go. Look at the graphics and how the categories on the page are arranged, and notice how you navigate deeper into the hierarchy of pages. Use the sites' features. Compare the way different sites work, look, and feel. Why are they different? What are the motivating philosophies behind the design, the voice, and the technological choices that went into their creation? Does your browser support everything they try to send you? Can you even tell?

How could they all be linked as a medium when the Web's flexibility lets sites serve so many different purposes? On one hand, some sites are a vast sea of information, organized rigidly with a strong sense of hierarchy: they're all about function. Others are a pure expression of artistry, with sparse information presented through a strong aesthetic sense: these are all about form.

Think of the two extremes as the *library* and the *gallery*.

The library has a vast collection of information available in numerous formats. It isn't concerned with the display of the information, just the method of organization. It expects that you know what kind of info you want, so its main goal is a clear, organized system to help you find what you want as quickly as possible. It doesn't necessarily put the best books closest to the front door; it doesn't open their pages to give you a peek.

Conversely, the gallery offers a controlled presentation of its artwork. It is a carefully orchestrated space designed to give every visitor the same, meticulously curated aesthetic experience.

The roles of each extreme are not interchangeable. It would be absurd to carve the words of all the books in the library into the walls of the building and elegantly light them for display. Likewise, stacking paintings in alphabetical order and letting visitors flip through for themselves would be pathetic.

Being clear on where your project fits on the library-gallery continuum is the first step toward successfully navigating the maze of compromises and tough questions that working on the Web will demand of you. The goal is to balance pure information with an aesthetic that not only complements the message but also becomes part of the voice.

## A little history: the Web's roots

The Web has evolved into an exceptionally flexible medium – one that accommodates the full spectrum between gallery and library. But when it started out, it was just the opposite.

Oddly enough, the reason the form-function question is so important in electronic publishing is that, in the medium's beginning, the architects of the World Wide Web sought to remove that balance entirely. Their goal was a radical one: to completely separate form and function, thereby creating a simple publishing system that would cross all platforms and be independent and portable.

Their answer was hypertext markup language. HTML was created to let documents travel across the Web with minimal baggage: only simple labels would separate their parts. Early HTML allowed creators to mark what was <BODY>a page </BODY>, <H1>a headline</H1>, <P>a paragraph</P>, <H4>a subhead<H4>, and so on. When the document reached its destination, the internal rules of the viewer's browser (such as "display headlines as 18-point bold type") would take over, showing the document in a format appropriate to the machine and the user.

This concept of separating an element's function from its appearance is pretty abstract for designers trained in print publishing (and most of the rest of us too). It's not at all like using popular desktop publishing programs such as Adobe PageMaker. With PageMaker, a designer chooses to display some text in, say, 30-point Helvetica, in an exact shade of process color, in an absolute position on the page. Seeing type with those characteristics on the finished page, the reader instinctively knows she's reading a headline. The designer has communicated "headline" straight to the reader, without ever telling the application that that's what 30-point Helvetica and the other specifications mean. It's a one-step process. The designer uses the application as a tool to visually communicate the document's structure to the reader.

HTML adds a step. The designer tells the document what its parts are. But the communication is really between the vast array of browsers and readers – wresting away much of the designer's control.

Of course, when you try to design with a system like this, traditional rules that apply in the print world fail miserably. Designers who are accustomed to precise typographic control are stunned when they realize the degree to which their work can differ from machine to machine when they design for the Web.

### So long, ivory tower

Why would the early pioneers of the Web design such a limiting system of publishing? One answer only: compatibility. Their goal was to create a language that would allow anyone to publish a document that would be readable by any sort of device – a high-end workstation with a twenty-inch monitor, a dumb terminal on a mainframe, a handheld computer, or a braille output system. The same document would be able to gracefully adapt – or degrade – to the constraints of any display device, no matter how many colors it could show or what fonts were installed. The Web's creators envisioned systems that could read HTML documents aloud, emphasizing headings and pausing between paragraphs. It was the genesis of the world's virtual library.

This philosophy was elegant and graceful but not realistic. First, the creators of the Web never anticipated that their project would be used for anything beyond basic text-based documents. It was a system designed so that researchers studying high-energy particle physics could trade, publish, and review their work. Within that context, nearly all documents were similar in structure, appearance, and use. Today's Web, of course, is vastly different from the ivory-tower tool of years ago. All sorts of users are online and have carved out niches on the Web – from publishing empires to digital artists and the keepers of Shakespeare. How can a simple structural language accommodate such a wide variety of publishing applications? It can't. Take, for example, the evolutionary changes Netscape and Microsoft have made to HTML. With the addition of tags like <FONT> and <MARQUEE>, designers have been given more control over their pages but at the cost of diluting the language. The Web – and HTML in particular – has mushroomed into something unrecognizable as that early simple system because it has had to respond to the demands of traditional publishing aesthetics.

The creators of the Web also failed to anticipate that dozens of browsers would soon sprout up for every computing platform, each with its own way of presenting the Web's structural documents. Each browser used its own set of style rules for each element on a page. And naturally, those style rules were developed by the engineers who wrote the browsers. Those engineers were the same ones who decided that 11-point Times with solid leading on a 23 percent gray background was as legible as text ever needed to be. They continued to advance their browser technology, but the crucial functionality that designers needed was never a priority. Browsers developed cool 3-D plug-ins and streaming digital video long before anyone could control something as fundamental to design as typefaces. But slowly, the design community's voice is being heard in the online publishing world.

**What's out there**

The balance between form and function is everywhere on the Web. Every site you visit lines up with the rest on a continuum between library and gallery. Let's start with two examples at the extremes: the sprawling Web directory Yahoo and the powerful experimental art site jodi.

*structure*                                    *presentation*

**Library**                                    **Gallery**

Yahoo may be the quintessential example of an online library. The über-directory of Web sites does manage to convey style and attitude, but underlying that is a simple, highly structured hierarchy of information. This emphasis on structure and function over presentation is appropriate for a reference site like Yahoo. Still, that gray background is a relic.

The beauty of sticking to pure structure in Web design is embodied in Yahoo's transparent clarity for users and portability across browsers. By keeping the content purely logical, the site focuses on its usefulness as an information database. This database can be displayed in any number of

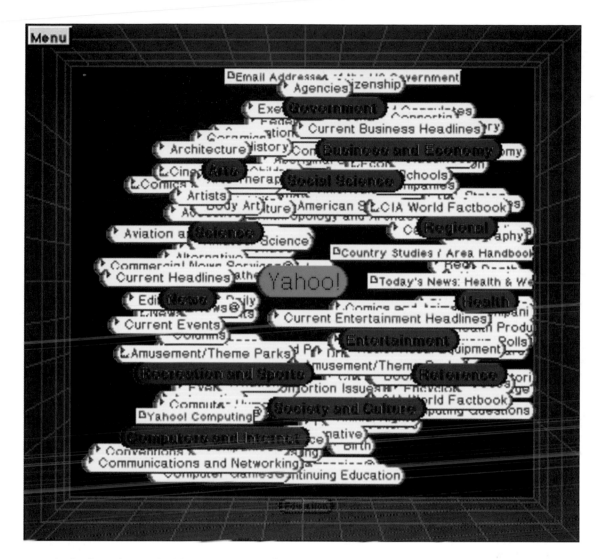

ways, including the typical browser example opposite. Yahoo
exploits the technology of the Web for its
distribution abilities, not for its interactive, graphical qualities.

By relying on HTML's most basic functions, Yahoo's
creators have maximized the number of ways to display data.
Yahoo works just fine in a text-only browser such as Lynx,
just as it will display easily on a television browser like WebTV.
Nascent technologies like Apple's HotSauce, which lets
users fly through Yahoo's categories and lists in 3-D space,
work well too. The seemingly infinite list of Web sites is
Yahoo's most crucial element, but it's *the information about
the information* – the metadata – that makes the content
portable, malleable, and accessible.

*Embrace the Medium*

  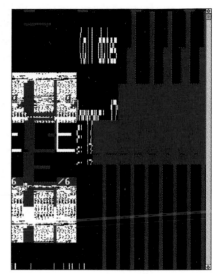

At the other extreme, jodi.org is pure creativity – an online gallery. This site's substance *is* style. Don't look here for hierarchy, structure, a site map, or even clear navigational elements. Instead, each page offers an *experience*: you, the viewer, move through a visual amalgam of color, shape, and motion into increasingly complex and stunning work. The authors have created a pure vision, pushing far past the constraints of the medium to exploit the liabilities of the Web and HTML. This site, of course, has its own structure, but visitors don't need to learn the interface or visualize the site layout. They just take in the visual stimulation streaming by.

The Web has evolved far beyond the vision of its original architects. While the technology has blazed ahead, pushed by corporations like Netscape, Sun, and Microsoft, the true innovation has come from the other end of the wire. Since the Web as a design medium is an ever-changing matrix of possibility and limitation, the point is to determine where on the continuum between library and gallery your content sits and then to create a clear, bold, and well-designed solution to your set of problems.

Take a look at how some successful sites have handled these issues.

## Background Check

Background images can be a powerful way of presenting a visual hierarchy. Though HTML offers no ability to layer information, a background can serve as an organizational structure, allowing you to separate content and navigation, for example. In the *CNN Interactive* example, the designers have specified a thin horizontal strip with gray and white areas as their background image; the browser then tiles this image down the page, creating the gray bar on the left. The syntax is simple: `<BODY BACK­GROUND="foo.gif">`. But be careful: the image wraps both horizontally *and* vertically. Widen your window enough and the gray bar in the CNN example shows up again on the right. To prevent this type of unintended wraparound, make your background image at least 800 pixels wide.

### East Timor democracy leaders named Nobel Peace Prize winners

(AP Photo)

All acquitted in apartheid-era massacre

1996 Nobel Peace Prize winners
(AP Photo/file)

Pro-democracy advocate Jose Ramos-Horta and Roman Catholic Bishop Carlos Filipe Ximenes Belo of East Timor won the Nobel Peace Prize Friday for their efforts in that troubled former Portuguese colony.

**FULL STORY**

- Gaetti tomahawks the Braves, NLCS tied 1-1
- Orioles trip Yankees 5-3 to even ALCS 1-1

CONTENTS
HELP!
FEEDBACK

DEMOCRACY IN America
They Don't Bake Cookies
ON AIR

Baseball PLAYOFFS
LINK OF THE DAY

To keep up with every nail-biting here. We've got all playoff game, click here. We've got all the bases covered.

excite
Search the Web
SEARCH CNN
SEARCH

THE NEW PATHFINDER
YOUR HOME ON THE NET
PATHFINDER

DIGEST

ALMANAC

VIDEO VAULT

newsQuiz
SPECIALS

What's on TV
ON AIR

GUIDE TO CNN Networks

## TOP STORIES

### U.S.

- Post office sets deadlines for Christmas mail
- Two arrested in freeway sniper attacks
- Pentagon delays Gulf War
- O.J.'s friend says he doubts Simpson's innocence
- In other news...

### ALLPOLITICS

- Dole cuts Clinton's lead again in California
- Head games in Virginia Senate ad draw fire

### SCI-TECH

- Site seer: That research paper was due when?
- Popularity of late physicist revived on Internet

### SHOWBIZ

- Sony character 'crashes' mainstream game market
- Drama critic Walter Kerr dies

### STYLE

- Versace spring 97: Soft, sweet and vulnerable

### FEEDBACK

- Tell us what you think!
- You said it...

### NEWS PAGER

- Shockwave pager - Get the latest news through your pager

### WORLD

- British soldier dies from Monday's IRA bomb
- Muslims delay mosque opening to avoid clash with Israelis
- In other news...

### CNNfn

- McDonald's opens in India
- China bans some U.S. fowl
- China to lift fund freeze
- Time-TBS merger final
- Current stock quotes

### SPORTS

- NFL fines Cox $87,500 for obscene gesture
- Baseball scoreboards - NL | AL
- Edberg knocks Muster from CA Trophy tourney
- NHL Scoreboard

### HEALTH

- Nasal spray for allergies may soon be sold in stores
- Doctor offers addicts 'rapid' way off heroin

### EARTH

- Australia declares war on pesky rabbits

### JOB OPENING

- Check out the latest job opening at CNN Interactive, the leading provider of interactive news.

Back to the top

**CNN Interactive** <www.cnn.com>: While the CNN Web site is largely based on the functional library model, it pulls away from the extreme by borrowing some of the gallery model's design values. Although the site is, in fact, a vast library of past and present news stories, a strong emphasis on visuals and multimedia makes today's stories dramatic and vivid. A good example for electronic news editions, *CNN Interactive* serves as both a graphical window into today's breaking headlines and a door to a digital archive of information.

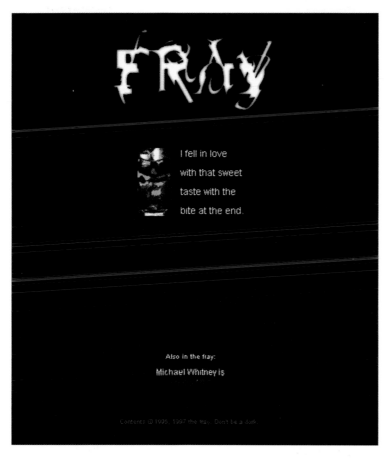

*Just Mousing Around*
By incorporating JavaScript mouseOver events with section listings, the fray <www.fray.com> adds interactivity to its pages and creates a compelling navigational experience. The individual icons appear to come alive under the user's mouse. The technique involves sensing when the mouse passes over an icon and replacing that image with another, precached icon from an array. You can get a good introduction to the JavaScript language at Netscape's site <home.netscape.com/eng/mozilla/3.0/ handbook/javascript/index.html>.

**the fray** <www.fray.com>: Since Designer Derek Powazek envisioned his Web project, the fray, as an expression of his philosophy that personal storytelling is the essence of the Web, it logically followed that he closely adhered to the gallery model. Using a dark atmosphere and an unpretentious graphic style, he developed click-through stories that gave visitors a sense of getting into the minds of the featured authors. The site explores different pacing and

**Like the way search.com allows you to search other engines from its pages? You can do the same thing. To add HotBot's search interface to one of your pages, use the following code:**

```
<FORM ACTION="http://www.hotbot.com/" NAME="HSQ">
<TABLE CELLPADDING="0" CELLSPACING="0" BORDER="0">
<TR><TD COLSPAN="4">
    <TABLE CELLPADDING="0" CELLSPACING="2" BORDER="0">
    <TR><TD>SEARCH</TD>
    <TD><SELECT NAME="SW">
        <OPTION VALUE="web" SELECTED>the Web
        <OPTION VALUE="usenet">Usenet News
    </SELECT></TD></TR><TR></TR>
    <TR><TD>for</TD>
    <TD><SELECT NAME="SM">
        <OPTION VALUE="MC" SELECTED >all the words
        <OPTION VALUE="SC">any of the words
        <OPTION VALUE="phrase">the exact phrase
        <OPTION VALUE="name">the person
        <OPTION VALUE="url">links to this URL
        <OPTION VALUE="B">the Boolean expression
    </SELECT></TD></TR>
    </TABLE>
<INPUT TYPE="hidden" NAME="MOD" VALUE="0">
<P>
<INPUT TYPE="hidden" NAME="DC" VALUE="10">
<INPUT TYPE="hidden" NAME="DE" VALUE="10" VALUE="2">
<P>
Enter query:
<INPUT TYPE="text" VALUE="" SIZE="40" NAME="MT" MAXLENGTH="100">
<INPUT TYPE="submit" NAME="act.search" VALUE="Search">
<INPUT TYPE="hidden" NAME="OPs" VALUE="R">
<INPUT TYPE="hidden" NAME="_v" VALUE="2">
</TD>
</TR>
</TABLE>
</FORM>
```

flow in the individual stories, while still maintaining a consistent sense of authorship. But unlike pure gallery sites such as jodi, the fray provides a simple, hierarchical navigational structure for the various sections of content. The site confidently exploits a number of new technologies but does so in a quiet, unassuming way. By controlling the user's experience, the fray makes its content, not its style, the main attraction.

**search.com** <www.search.com>: Although CNET's search.com is a colorful and somewhat visually active site, it actually falls at the extreme library end of the spectrum because every decision and element is in the service of pure function. As part of the CNET network of Web sites <www.cnet.com>, search.com inherits a look and feel from its family. So the CNET logo and ubiquitous yellow stripe are practical elements in the extreme. They may be GIFs, but they do the work of branding and orientation. This serves search.com well, because the site is first and foremost a utility – a tool for users looking for information on the Web.

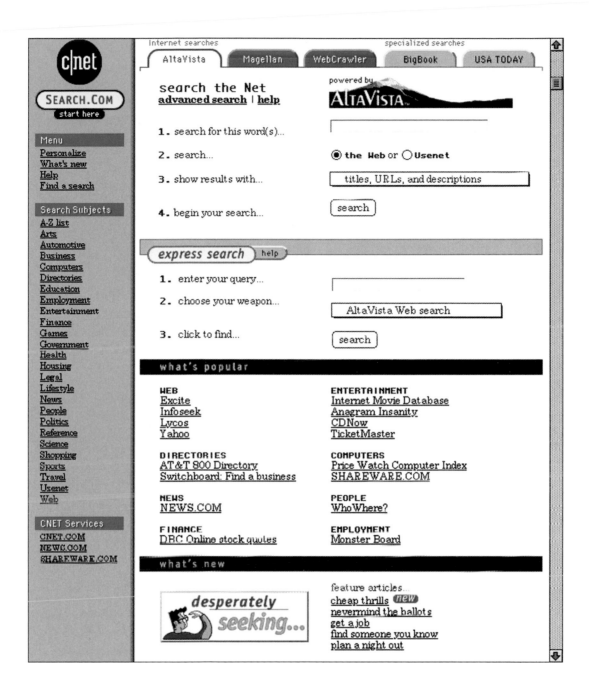

To design for the Web is to inhabit a strange space where today's demands (eye-catching visuals and engaging interactivity) are hampered by yesterday's priorities (portability and reusability), and clever compromise is your best friend.

Your site will undoubtedly fall somewhere between the extremes of function and style. But by learning to see the medium for what it is, you can take control of the trade-offs you'll have to make in creating your site, letting the Web's limitations sharpen your focus rather than ensure your downfall.

# New Thinking for a New Medium: The Evolution of HotWired's Frontdoor

When HotWired launched in 1994, it was one of the first commercial sites to create editorial content especially for the Web. Our motto, New Thinking for a New Medium, was not just something for our press releases. New Thinking for a New Medium was our working philosophy. It made us cast off models ingrained in us from our print, broadcast, and software development backgrounds.

Embarking on this journey into the unknown, we faced all the difficulties inherent in creating Web sites today, but we had few models from which to draw inspiration or wisdom. The history of HotWired's homepage – what we call our frontdoor – is ultimately the story of our own efforts to balance form and function in this limited and evolving medium.

### "I love it! What is it?": The premiere frontdoor

We may have imagined a textured, vibrant, multimedia Web site brimming with style and attitude, but our October 1994 frontdoor was an exquisite exercise in creative frustration. We went live on the Net a month before Netscape released the first version of its Navigator browser. At that time, most of the layout options we take for granted on the Web today – background colors, image aligning, centered text, and font sizes, just to name a few – didn't exist. Back then, designers heard one mantra from engineers: "No, you can't do that – it isn't possible." By necessity, we learned to exploit the Web's idiosyncrasies.

HotWired's premiere frontdoor must have stunned surfers in those early Web days of nothing but text-heavy, gray Web pages. Just one large image map showing stylish icons for each of the site's five sections, this design elegantly expressed the aesthetic of our site. But its functionality was minimal, to say the least. The page's sparse simplicity gave visitors few clues to the scope of the sections behind the icons. And the long download times and latency of the Net at that time made asking visitors to explore our site – to wander blindly through it – an act of naïve delusion.

Of course, we thought the site made perfect sense: the structure was hierarchical, with each icon on the frontdoor leading to the frontdoor of one of our sections (or as we called them "channels"). From there, users could choose individual features ("programs"), which often started out with another frontdoor type page. Thus, to get to HotWired 1.0 content, a user would load the front page, choose a section like Renaissance, load up another whole page, then choose a program like Retina, load that whole page, and then begin reading content.

We had to shift gears – to be faster – if we wanted to put our work in front of readers.

While our first frontdoor was winning design awards, visitors were complaining that they couldn't find anything. After all, a homepage on the Web might be the portal to a dozen other pages or a thousand or – who's to know? Unlike a book or a magazine, whose thickness, weight, and conventional table of contents tell the reader what to expect, a Web site's frontdoor requires the designer to provide clues about the site's depth and focus to readers.

Virtually no typographic control was available on the Web at that time, so if we wanted to make something striking and visually compelling for our frontdoor, graphics were our only option. But our designers were appalled to learn that if an image was a link to other content, it would automatically be enclosed by a 2-point-thick, bright blue border. Our engineers told us that it was the only way people would know they were to follow a link. Placing more faith in our users, the designers took this design "bug" and made it a feature, creating our own chunky, offset border in bright blue around frontdoor graphics. When we made interface elements like the Coin icon bleed out over the borders, we were consciously integrating the browser-supplied outlines into our visual scheme.

This strategy – making the Web's limitations serve our interests – became the foundation of our development philosophy. We couldn't exploit the best of the medium without it.

Settling on an all-graphics page, though, meant we were entering the dangerous territory of clunky, slow-loading pages that visitors leave out of impatience. So we restricted the color palette as much as possible, eventually ending up with just eight colors. The double-edged promise and demands of image compression made us create chunky, coarsely drawn images so that our visually big, bold graphics compressed down into small files.

**Frontdoor two**

Our next version sought to add function to the pure form and style that had dominated the premiere frontdoor. Striving to make our navigation clear and explicit, we basically made a text map of the site and put it on the front page below a modified version of our original icon bar.

That way, text did some of the page's communication work and made for a quicker download. We had simplified our icons even further, sucking more color from the image. The new four-color scheme carried on the essence of the first frontdoor but shifted the emphasis of the page to navigation, not aesthetics.

For the page's text list of channels and programs, we began to play with some extremely limited typographic techniques using the HTML <PRE> tag (preformatted text), which allowed our designers to align text by using a monospaced font. For more detail and a sense of freshness, we incorporated three text blurbs about new content at the top of the page. These little teasers were written by our editors and put into a database, where they'd be pulled out by scripts that our engineers wrote to count characters in each line, space the teasers accordingly, and rotate their appearance on the site.

Below the central image, we again used preformatted text to list the entire contents of our Web site and links to every program. The result was usable but also overwhelming. Where we once had five links, we now presented our users with two dozen. And there still was no explanation of what waited behind the links.

This front-page map also flattened HotWired's site structure. Now we were no longer constrained to the rigid hierarchy of our first site so our users no longer needed to navigate through layers of pages to get to content. It was now a two-step process: use the homepage, load a content page – totally eliminating the channel homepages. It was difficult to get lost now, but as the site grew, it was getting tougher to know where to go and why.

To help individual users find their way through the site, we began to personalize each user's view. Since our Web site required users to enter a name and a password when they visited, we were able to use a database to keep track of which programs on our site they had seen and which they had not. Each time a user returned, a server-side script would ask the database for the pertinent info and then dynamically show content the user hadn't yet seen in boldface with the explanation, "What's New."

But as you can imagine, we weren't satisfied with the flatness of the page and just listing the often cryptic names of our many features. As new technologies emerged, we began to add flair back into our now useful but primitive frontdoor.

## Frontdoor three

As the Web's speed and our readers' equipment and connections improved, we felt less compelled to make the frontdoor an easy entrance to every part of the site. Once again, we could aim for our aesthetic goals: style, freshness, attitude. So we swung back toward form over function. In this iteration, our utterly overwhelming frontdoor lost its links as navigation moved deeper into the site onto a separate What's New page. We replaced the crude text teasers with a trio of colorful images, cut in our trademark "rakish" angles and still serving as links, since advances in HTML allowed us to hide those old-fashioned blue borders. These images were still being pulled from a database with a pool of teasers, but they were such a dominant element of the page that our frontdoor appeared to change each time a user visited. Additional intelligence was built into the rotating teasers, as well. Now, editors could indicate the priority level for individual teasers as they added them to the database. If a special feature or live event needed more attention, we could make it appear more often on the seemingly random pages. Older content could be shuffled

### Border Patrol

We couldn't control the image borders when we first built HotWired, but that situation has certainly changed. Among the additions to HTML over the years is the BORDER attribute in the `<IMG>` tag. You can now use the image border attribute cleverly to control the look of your graphics. The syntax is simple:

`<IMG SRC="foo.gif" BORDER="0">`
 produces no border

`<IMG SRC="foo.gif" BORDER="2">`
 produces the standard border

`<IMG SRC="foo.gif" BORDER="10">`
 produces a chunky, 10-point border

You can set the color of the border by changing the page's LINK attribute in the `<BODY>` tag.

The cascading style sheet (CSS) specification allows for even more control. Authors can add a border to any element and specify its style (solid, dashed, beveled, or others) as well as color and width. For more about style sheets, see "Many Pages, One Style," on page 35.

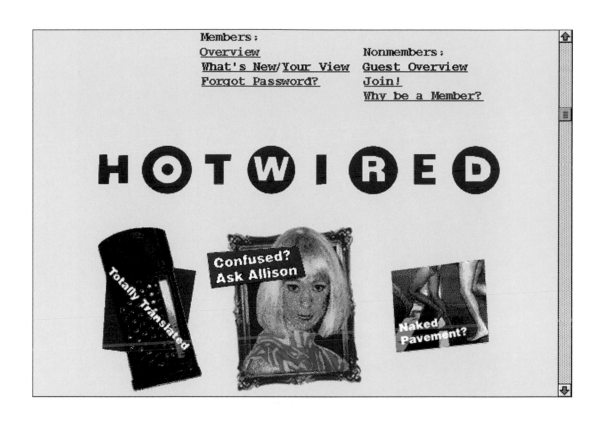

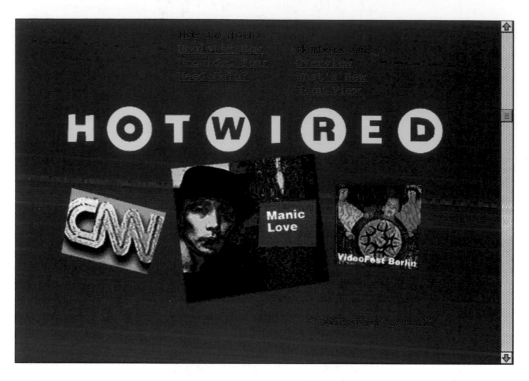

into the mix as well, but with lower priorities, creating a wide range of choices with the attention on new content.

The most dramatic change, however, was the vibrant background color that became a HotWired standard. A new addition to HTML let us place a tiling image behind our pages, and we picked the brightest entries in our color palette, following on the aesthetics of our offline sibling, *Wired* magazine. So with each return to HotWired, our visitors saw a different color as a script randomly grabbed a different background with the refresh of the page. Combining that with the rotating image teasers, HotWired seemed to reinvent itself continuously.

The drawback to this flashy new welcome for visitors was that we removed nearly all of the functionality of the previous homepage. The What's New feature and site map were now pushed down a level into their own pages. The third frontdoor acted exclusively as a gateway to visitors, leading them either to a few select pieces of highlighted content or to a sitewide index. This was an exciting entryway to HotWired, setting a tone and introducing the site's personality to the visitor. But users were again disoriented in our vast site and needed more help getting to know our channels and programs.

*Changing Colors*

When we added the random background color to HotWired's frontdoor, we did so by creating separate versions of the page and placing them on different Web servers. Visitors would get assigned to a random server when reaching our site and would get the illusion of a dynamically generated page. Today, however, the same effect could be accomplished in your audience's browser by using a scripting language. JavaScript's *document.bgcolor* property can be simply tweaked to a different color each time a page is loaded. Much simpler, much faster.

### Frontdoor four

The next version of HotWired's frontdoor blended together the previous versions. Our lurid color palette remained, and the background color continued to rotate with each visit. We used both text and image teasers, again served up randomly. And the navigation links returned in a limited form, now as grouped icons, names, and short descriptions of our channels. More detailed navigation now lived on a separate interface level, and we pointed to it from the top of the page.

Behind the scenes, this front page was rigidly defined in a templated grid of structural information, navigation, and content teasers and was almost entirely generated on the fly with each new visitor. Images and colors and links were all poured into the template by complex back-end scripts.

But although the results were fluid, our template was rigid. Still, our frontdoor couldn't react to breaking news. And it was nearly impossible to play around with new ideas or to go in new directions in electronic publishing. While we were comfortable with the balance we'd reached among navigation, graphic art, and information display, we felt the need to explore beyond our template-based homepage and to begin experimenting with what we – and the Web – were capable of.

**Monday, 24 Feb 97**

Webmonkey
The Netizen
Packet
Dream Jobs
Brain Tennis
Surf Central
Test Patterns
Cocktail
Ask Dr. Weil
Rough Guide
Piazza
Threads

WIRED
Wired News
Magazine
Wired Source

talk.com

Tools
Launch Toolbar

**HOTWIRED AFTER HOURS**

From Han Solo to streaming audio, here's what we do while the rest of the world sleeps. In Test Patterns.

**WHAT GETS CUT**

Attach rate: A black Magic Marker for business plans that would otherwise run red. Ned Brainard, in Flux.

**REBECCA VESELY, IN THE NETIZEN**

The CDA saga continues, as anti-censorship forces file briefs asking that the Supreme Court uphold the Act's reversal.

**DIGITAL NEWS FEED**

If you want to feel the Force, shop around: Your chances of seeing *The Empire Strikes Back* in a THX theater are about 50/50. In Wired News.

**IN THE NETIZEN**

While affluent Americans kvetch about online perils, Katz hears firsthand how the world at large hungers for the Net.

**PUSHES AND FLOWS**

Is push media the next wave of the digital revolution, or the death knell of Web culture? The debate begins, in Brain Tennis.

**CAPTIVE AUDIENCE**

It's not that Netscape's new Kiosk mode is addictive - you just won't be able to quit! In Webmonkey.

Get a free issue of
*Wired* magazine.

**Whadya** think?
Dive into our archive.

Get HotWired or
Wired News delivered
daily to your desktop!

**Frontdoor five**

This time we retained from the previous frontdoor all the balances we'd achieved: between text and images, between updates and consistency. But we shifted the emphasis from the sections of HotWired to the new content in those sections, which was changing daily. This page consisted largely of a series of text blurbs and images that encapsulated the day's offerings. Far more labor-intensive than any of our previous schemes, this plan required a dedicated staff to write and design it each day. For the first time, this daily HotWired page served not only as a tool for using our site but as an effective guide to the ideas, news, and features we were presenting that day. We had stopped making visitors guess what might appeal to them and gave them enough information to choose specific destinations.

Overall site navigation was now relegated to a narrow strip of channel images in a left-hand column. Section descriptions were dropped, shifting the emphasis from a channel's ongoing mission to what it offered right now. The top of the right column prominently displayed the date, showing users how frequently the page was updated. And in keeping with the daily emphasis, the background color was no longer randomly chosen but instead rotated among five colors, each of which was assigned to one weekday.

Remembering the powerful scene-setting effect of those colorful, entertaining introductory pages in the third frontdoor, we began producing a series of dramatic animated teasers that popped up when people went to <www.hotwired.com> and then led them to our homepage. These funny, colorful little spots were dubbed *splashes* and served a variety of purposes. They highlighted and promoted one new feature every day, using a visual style and a sense of humor that added coherence to our site. And they were clever and innovative enough to make visitors come back every day just to see what we'd come up with.

Splashes had to be simple – one animation running for five to ten seconds over a solid background, then automatically jumping to the frontdoor. This became an area of intense creativity and exploration for designers: they pushed to communicate a focused message while fighting bandwidth constraints and primitive browser technology. For a case study in splashes, see "Splashing Down" on page 102. A collection of splashes is at <www.hotwired.com/frontdoor/archive/>.

## Frontdoor six

HotWired's frontdoor was closer to our ideal of building a daily relationship with our readers, yet it still lacked some of the key features we had been striving for. Although we could now emphasize different content ideas through the splashes and teaser copy, we were still forced to flow everything into the same rigid layout.

We could see a way out of this rigidity, however. As we planned our next redesign, browser developers began demonstrating what they were convinced would be the Next Big Thing in Web publishing – dynamic HTML. Soon, these developers argued, our designers would be able to move and replace elements on their pages with the same power afforded to CD-ROM publishing, thus enabling the fluidity we desired. Most of these early attempts, however, consisted of merely animating blocks of text to assemble when loaded.

We decided to take a step farther.

Using some of the techniques we had developed earlier - random background colors and mixing teasers - we added behaviors and attributes to individual elements. Each piece of our frontdoor, from the navigation bar to the HotWired logo and even advertisements, were scripted with a basic set of variables. Images would grow to fill empty spaces, text would stop moving when not overlapping, two objects with the same color would keep a balanced distance from one another. These elements could be embued with new attributes over time, building up a library of possible combinations to give the impression of constant activity, and allowing us to leave behind the static quality of earlier front doors. Our goal was a sort of scripted chaos. We began to think of our pages as a theatrical production.

While the possibilities were both exciting and liberating, the execution was often painful and frustrating. Our pages relied entirely on untested beta-version grade technology. Bugs abounded, and our editorial and design process had to be re-examined because our content was now interwoven with the scripting languages responsible for the dynamic experience.

Editors and designers, already comfortable with the collaboration required of them, were joined in the content loop by engineers. Words, pictures, and now code, were integrated into a seemless experience for our users.

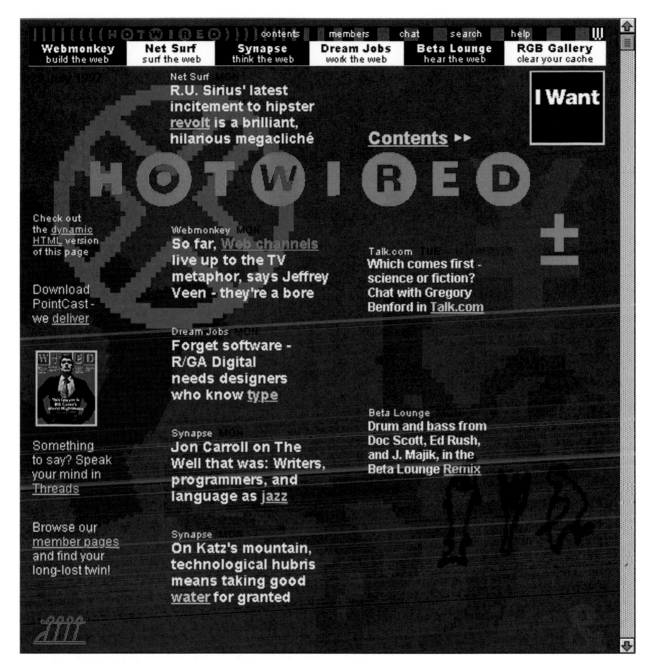

The lessons of the HotWired frontdoor: Fight limitations with innovation. Be fast and streamlined. Be bold and daring. Be clear and simple. Personalize views. Show what's new. And to do all this, master the technology.

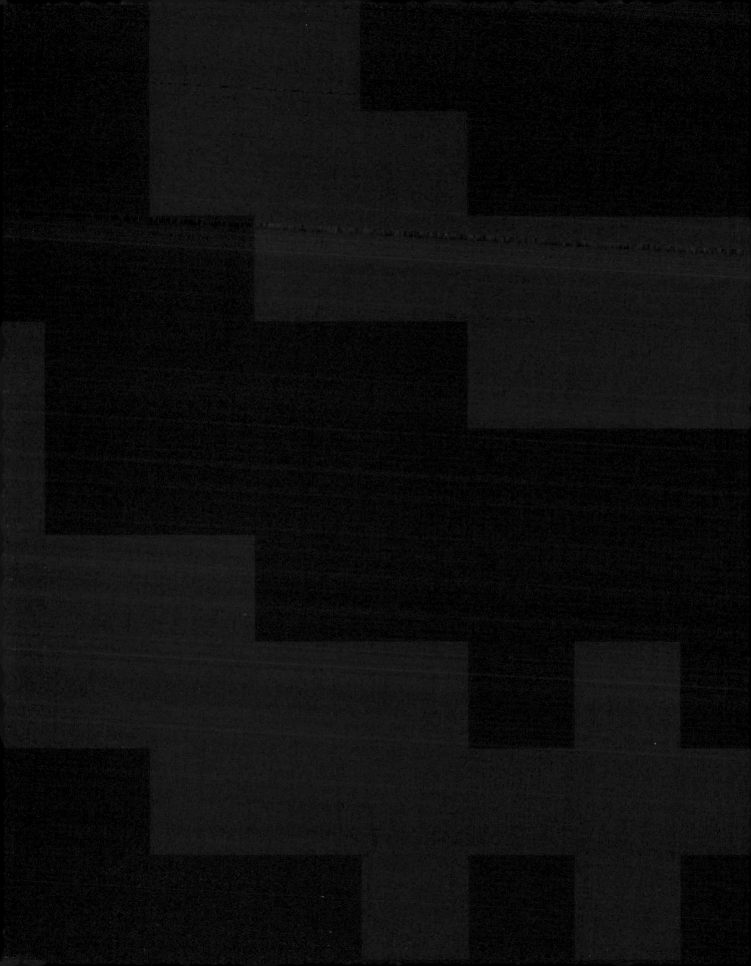

# Know Your Code

Oh, the power of technology. Remember the desktop publishing "revolution" back in the eighties? Everyone with PageMaker and a Mac could make slick-looking brochures, newsletters, and reports. And everyone did, with dreadful results. Dozens of typefaces competed with ghastly clip art.

Powerful tools are no substitute for skill and experience.

It's the same in any medium. Video students fill their first projects with exploding starburst transitions; photography buffs can drown in a sea of gadgets, all offering to "enhance" their pictures. Without a doubt, the Web has offered the same fertile ground for abuse: blinking text, fractal backgrounds, and rendered 3-D buttons compete for attention on homepages across the Net.

But there is a difference online. The Web is *so* new and *so* everchanging that designers have to digest each innovation with each new browser release. Design trends on the Web can be measured in weeks, as the hype of new capabilities filters through the screens. So Web-site creation isn't something you learn once and then check off on your to do list. It's an ongoing learning process – you're always susceptible to gratuitous, trite uses of new features.

Your job is to find balance. Given the hyperspeed development of the Web, jumping on every new trick is as bad as burying your head in the sand. The right decisions are the ones that fit your content. Is it closer to the library or gallery end of the continuum? Or does it fall somewhere between the two? The technologies you use and the features you exploit should serve your site's basic goals.

Your journey starts at the beginning, of course, by learning HTML. Don't be intimidated. HTML is an easy, straightforward markup language. You don't have to be a programmer to learn it. Children – and even management – pick it up quickly.

So dive in. The one and only way to seize control of publishing on the Web is to know your code.

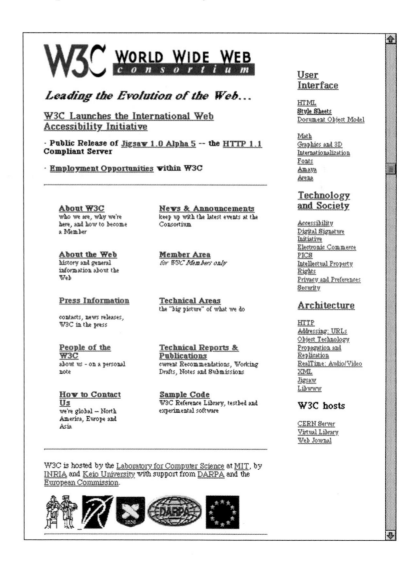

## Toss the how-tos

The best way to learn the specifics of building Web pages is from the Web itself. Any HTML how-to book out there could be a good introduction to marking up documents, but the language is changing as fast as technology. Trying to keep printed books up-to-date with HTML's evolution is like trying to drink from a fire hose. There's too much too fast to get it all.

But the constantly updated Web is the perfect resource. You can start by going to the experts. The World Wide Web Consortium <www.w3.org>, also known as W3C, is the keeper of standards for the Web community. On its Web site, you can find the official specifications for all Web-based languages and formats, as well as reports and drafts of future work. The site also contains hypertext guides and a virtual library of electronic publishing resources.

Webmonkey <www.webmonkey.com>, HotWired's online service station, takes advantage of the Web's interactivity to let readers ask staff members questions about HTML and then discuss the language and its uses among themselves. Webmonkey also offers tutorials, industry news, and pointers to other online resources.

But while sites like Webmonkey and W3C let you read *about* HTML, you'll learn the language best by reading HTML itself. Every browser gives you some way of viewing the source code of Web sites you visit. In Netscape's Navigator, for example, you can select Document Source from the View menu. As you surf the Web, watch for interesting page layouts. When you wonder how someone did something, take a look at the source code and find out.

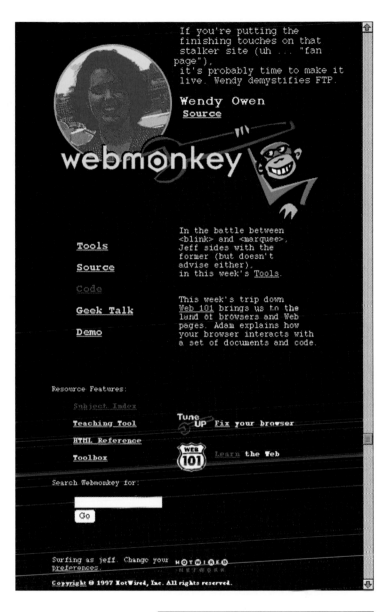

Although it's easy to do, of course you can't just copy and paste someone else's code into a document you're going to put live on the Web. As a learning tool, however, there is no better way to look over the shoulder of an experienced Web designer than to create dummy documents from found source code and play around with HTML.

## Ditch the editing software

With so many HTML editing software applications out there offering point-and-click Web page creation, you may wonder why you should even bother learning an arcane markup language. But using such software to automate making Web pages is no shortcut, because it won't take you where you want to go: to a deep understanding of HTML and

*Validation services*

*Validation services*
No matter how well you know your code, it's always a good idea to check it for glitches. Even the simplest pages can fester with hidden errors in the code and content. Add scripting languages, embedded media, or links to other sites, and you're bound to make a mistake or two. To help, several HTML validation services reside on the Web, including some that have been around since the early days.

**Weblint** <www.cre.canon.co.uk/~neilb/weblint/>: This technical, specific tool checks the validity of your code. Any errors in the syntax of your HTML will be pointed out – even the misuse of tags you may be using to hack a layout.

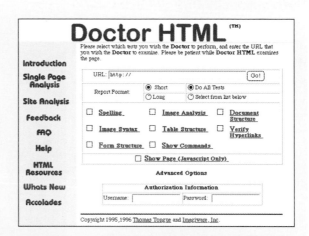

**Doctor HTML** <www2.imagiware.com/RxHTML/>: From this site, you can check not only your HTML syntax but your page's spelling as well. The Image Analysis feature is particularly useful: the script reports the image sizes as well as the estimated download time for an average user. Doctor HTML also checks out your links, makes sure your tables aren't a mess, and takes a look at your forms too.

**Bobby** <www.cast.org/bobby/>: This Web-based resource will find HTML compatibility problems that prevent pages from displaying correctly on different Web browsers. Type in a URL, select which browser you want to check it against, and off you go.

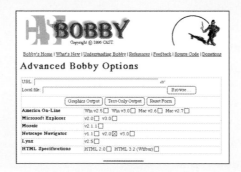

its uses. The problem is not with the software but with the very nature of HTML. When you try to author a document with an editor, either the software isn't powerful enough to assure compatibility with all browsers (try Adobe's PageMill), or it's so powerful that you have to know HTML inside and out to get it to fly (like SoftQuad's HoTMetaL Pro).

Each of the thousands of pages on HotWired were written by hand with either SimpleText or Bare Bones Software's BBEdit, and then tested on a dozen different browsers.

## Think like a hacker

Like everyone who has learned HTML before you, you'll be inspired by its possibilities and frustrated by its limitations. You already know that HTML's inventors didn't take into account the rich, integral graphics and complex layouts of today's Web when they formulated the language. The problem for designers, of course, is that each browser has a different set of rules for displaying HTML tags. The fact that the indentation for a <BLOCKQUOTE> tag has no uniform size across browsers, for example, is enough to make designers crazy.

But rather than give up in frustration, designers have responded to the Web's limitations in two ways.

The first – and mistaken – strategy that Web designers use to force a Web page to obey their aesthetic wishes involves breaking our first rule: Embrace the medium. Frustrated by the inability to make headlines and titles consistent across browsers, some designers just ignore the browsers' role. For a stylized headline, for example, they make a GIF graphic of the headline's words in the font, color, and style of their choice, and just place the images on the Web page as they would any other image. Unfortunately, this ensures that only human readers can decode the meaning of what is usually the most important text of the document. Unlike pages that a designer creates with plain HTML text, these pages aren't searchable or flexible enough to be accessible to a vast and diverse audience. These designers are, in essence, bypassing their translators. They are trying desperately to speak directly to their audience by clinging to the old rules of the print world, but by doing so, they seriously limit their audience.

The other – more skillful – design strategy takes more

*Shovel at Your Own Risk*
**Embracing the medium means almost always building your pages manually. Many converters exist, claiming to take your existing documents from Word, Quark XPress, or whatever and then to convert them into HTML. Don't be tempted. Unless your existing content is incredibly simple and highly structured, the process will usually result in a mess. Someday, sure, everybody will easily swap documents across platforms, but for now the conversion process is your responsibility. You won't get away with shoveling from one format to another.**

thought but is truer to the medium. It uses existing HTML in innovative ways to trick browsers into displaying complex layouts. The artful bastardization of HTML tables is a great example. Designed to allow tabular data (like spreadsheets) to be displayed in browsers, HTML's table tags offer a simple way of marking rows, data cells, and column headers. Page designers soon discovered, however, that certain extensions to the table specification would allow them to set margins, columns, and other layout devices they had learned to expect from desktop publishing programs.

Of course, structuralists thought that using a table for anything other than rows and columns of data was a corruption of the language. Designers and authors, however, considered it a simple way to exploit the medium without sacrificing elemental relationships on the page. It was a classic struggle between purity of form and purity of function. And the solutions, which were merely design hacks, bypassed the essence of the problem: HTML wasn't created with design control.

Remember: The browser is your ally. Let the browser know what is going on with your page by making text be text and images be images. Keep the browser in the communication loop, and keep your content independent from your layout dreams for it. Historically, this has meant sacrificing design control for structural flexibility, but things are about to change.

### Using Tables for Layout

Using tables for advanced Web page layout is de rigueur for most designers. Think of the page you are working on as if it were being displayed in a spreadsheet program like Microsoft Excel. You have rows and columns of cells. Now imagine placing

headlines, streams of copy, and images into those cells. Some cells overlap; others align in specified ways. In the illustrations above, you can see the grid we use to lay out our Netizen section. Before tables, this relatively straightforward layout would have been impossible.

### Finally, real control

In the early nineties, HTML was too limited to offer a suffi-cient tool set to professional designers. But only after years of earnest attempts at advanced design on the Web did a solution – style sheets – finally let designers break through the rigid display rules of each browser. Now, instead of anticipating the quirks in how each browser translates doc-uments, designers can send along their own translator with a document.

*The Single-Pixel GIF*
HTML workarounds, or kluges, have always been the pen and ink of Web designers. Invisible images are strategical-ly placed to push text from the edge of the screen in an attempt to position elements and create advanced layouts. Especially devoted emigrants from the print world have refused to acknowledge HTML's lack of leading control and used tiny vertical images on each line of type to space paragraphs.

The beauty of the single-pixel GIF hack is that you only need to create one image. Just use a graphics program like Photoshop to make a transparent GIF with the dimensions 1x1 pixels. Then, when you'd like to position elements on your page precisely, you can call in the GIF with the < IMG> tag, and specify whatever height and width you need – the browser will stretch the image to fit.

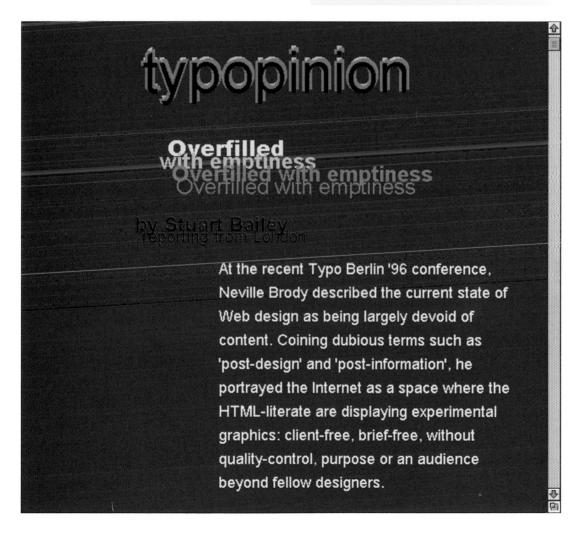

*Think like a hacker*

Style sheets let Web designers simply mark up text and images with basic structural tags in an HTML file and then send with the file a list of commands telling browsers how to interpret the tags. A style sheet might, for example, tell browsers which font, size, color, and spacing to use whenever they see <H1>. So the designer who once used graphics as a workaround for her purple script headlines can now get those same headlines on advanced browsers, but search engines and text-only browsers will also be able to read them.

Style sheets aren't limited to visuals. They also let designers control the action and timing on a Web page, opening possibilities for narrative and drama. Just as a browser has rules for rendering pages visually, it also has rules for rendering the behavior of pages. Typically, these rules are so simple, they don't even seem like rules. Read a headline, render a headline; read a paragraph, render a paragraph. However, putting the rules of each page element's behavior under a document author's control immediately opens up a world of dynamic content. Using a client-side scripting language (like Netscape's JavaScript), a page designer can begin to explore temporal design – making pages that evolve over time or react to a user's input. For example, headlines can move into position first, with body copy entering the screen moments later. Or items can turn on and off when a user clicks on a button.

Using style sheets is an advanced way of keeping design independent of content and structure (and as a way to keep both of them away from the underlying code), you enter a world of flexibility. Look at the benefits: You can offer your content in different styles based on what your audience is using to read your pages. Pages viewed on a screen, for example, can have different color values from those printed in black and white. Content also can outlive your designs. You can change typefaces in a quick edit. Site maintenance becomes a lot simpler. And you realize your ultimate goal: clear lines of communication among you, the browser, and your audience – regardless of hardware, software, or accessibility.

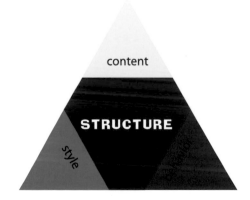

**Words, pictures, and code are the three elements that define the Web as a medium. Each is crucial; ignoring any one fails to exploit the unique nature of the Web. But each is also independent. If you make your content dependent on your design or page behavior, do it as conscious decision, not a result of poor planning or shallow design.**

**Do it because you know your code.**

This technology gets really interesting when you consider one style sheet with multiple content documents. Working with carefully designed pages, a designer can create a style sheet that encompasses an entire Web site. When changes are desired, simply editing the one style document updates the entire site automatically, or a new sheet can be quickly swapped in for an instant and complete site redesign. This cascading of style to multiple structured documents can span multiple sites in various locations.

The cascading style sheet (CSS) specification continues to evolve and advance. Designers now have control over exact positioning of elements, as well as the overlapping and layering of elements. You can specify the height and width of a paragraph, for example, and tell the browser to render that paragraph a certain distance from the top and left of the browser window. Thus, you can easily develop a grid-based system of page design, finally reserving HTML tables for their logical and intended purpose – rows and columns of data.

**raw content**

```
<H1>Finally,
real control</H1>
<P>In the early nineties,
HTML was too limited
to offer a sufficient
tool set to professional
designers. But only
after years of earnest
attempts at advanced
design on the Web did a
solution - style sheets -
finally let designers
break through the rigid
display rules of each
browser. Now, instead of
anticipating the quirks
in how each browser
translates documents,
designers can send along
their own translator
with a document.</P>
```

```
<H1>A little history:
the Web's roots</H1>
<P>The Web has evolved
into an exceptionally
flexible medium - one
that accommodates the
full spectrum between
gallery and library.
But when it started
out, it was just the
opposite.</P>
```

**style sheet**

```
<STYLE TYPE="text/css">
H1   {font: 8pt/9.5pt "Myriad Bold";}      Headline font: 8/9.5 Myriad Bold,
BODY {font: 8pt/9.5pt "Myriad";           Body font: 8/9.5 Myriad,
      margin: .25in .25in .25in .25in;    Margins: .25in all around
      backround-color: #FFFFFF;}          Backround color: white
</style>
```

**formatted text**

**A little history: the Web's roots**
The Web has evolved into an exceptionally flexible medium – one that accommodates the full spectrum between gallery and library. But when it started out, it was just the opposite.

**Finally, real control**
In the early nineties, HTML was too limited to offer a sufficient tool set to professional designers. But only after years of earnest attempts at advanced design on the Web did a solution – style sheets – finally let designers break through the rigid display rules of each browser. Now, instead of anticipating the quirks in how each browser translates documents, designers can send along their own translator with a document.

# Sacrificing Flexibility for Good Looks: The Rough Guides Online

When HotWired took on the project of putting the popular Rough Guide series of travel books online, we ran face-first into the dilemma forced on designers by the Web's separation of document structure and page presentation.

The organization of the books suggested a logical, hierarchical file structure (and therefore site structure) for their online counterparts. The world was divided into countries, then regions, states, cities. Even cities, finally, were divided – into passages telling you where to eat, where to sleep, and where to wander.

If you can imagine all of this content in the form of one massive document, the structure would be simple to describe using the most basic HTML. Top-level countries could be defined as <H1>, the most important heading. Further down in each nested group of files, regions would map to <H2>, states to <H3>, and likewise down the hierarchy. This simple site would facilitate pure communication.

*Know Your Code*

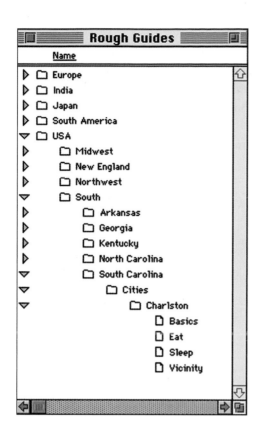

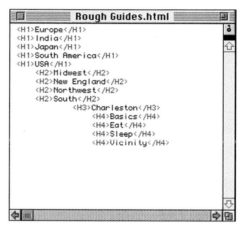

between the content and the browser, using the browser's default display settings. The page could be represented visually any number of ways – perhaps as a vanilla HTML document in which headers are set in increasingly smaller type, or perhaps in a browser's outline view based on the structure, with nested files and folders mapping to the levels of geographical detail.

Problem number one: HotWired isn't in the business of making vanilla, text-only Web pages. A purely structural presentation of the Rough Guides might have been effective as a portable, malleable electronic document, but frankly it would also have been visually primitive and veritably dull. Style was important. How to maintain the look and feel of the Rough Guides themselves, with their powerful brand image? How to create a compelling Web site with its own personality?

For starters, our designers tried image maps for each level of the hierarchy. Countries were shown with their names bound to their flags, and regional distinctions were overlaid on maps. The effect communicated a sense of navigation through geographical space.

Problem number two: By replacing text with images, we gave up the possibility that this content could be viewed with any other device beyond a graphical browser on a personal

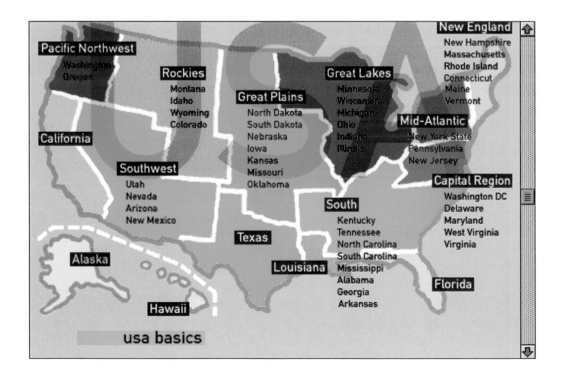

computer. We gave up on device-independent display – you wouldn't be able to browse this site on a wireless handheld device while wandering the streets of a foreign city. We also gave up on complete searchability, one of the most valuable advantages to using the Web to get travel info instead of relying on books.

The best solution, which was then unavailable, would have been to use style sheets to separate the design from the structure – to maintain the strict hierarchy of content via logical markup, while creating a visual identity that mapped to it. The <H1> text could be rendered in the Rough Guide font, DIN Schriften, overlaid on the appropriate flag GIF, with alignment and spacing characteristics built in. The navigational scheme at the regional level could remain as a collapsible outline of <H2> and <H3> rankings, but the style sheet could instruct the browser to place them in correct places on the map, again with typographical control remaining in the hands of the designer.

Style sheets would let the Rough Guide site look beautiful to Web surfers, would make it accessible to search engines, would keep it readable for text-only browsers, and would explicitly guide users through its hierarchical navigation. Without giving up style, structure, or clarity.

# Degrade Gracefully

It's every Web designer's worst nightmare. You've just finished the big project – you've created an amazing site for a very important client. Then you get The Call. Your client is frantic. The CEO just checked out the new Web site from home and – *gasp!* – couldn't get past the front page! You check the server and ask about the CEO's connection. Finally, the truth comes. He's using version 1.0 of AOL's browser. No Java, no JavaScript, no frames. He hasn't upgraded in months.

As far as the CEO is concerned, it's the site that's broken, not his antiquated system. You've got some work to do.

CEOs with old, feature-poor browsers are not your site's target audience, you may argue. But that is no excuse for sloppy, restrictive design. If your goal is a complex, technically sophisticated Web site, start with a solid, inclusive foundation that tells your message – independent of special effects.

First-time Web page authors almost never give a moment's thought to degradability. They mark up each page, checking it on their own machine and with their own browser, and when they like it, they stick it on their server and send it out to the Net's masses. Who cares about all those browsers that can't see their big graphics and multimedia tricks?

There are no "typical" Web users. Some will hit your page with the newest version of Netscape Navigator on a beefed-up multimedia PC fed by blazing T1 lines. Others will creep in over a modem, via AOL, on an old grayscale Mac IIci. Then there's the commuter who wants to check out your page on a wireless handheld computer, and the blind person whose computer reads your pages aloud. Given hardware differences, software upgrades, and monitor varieties, thousands of views of every page on the Web are possible.

Well-designed Web pages don't require high-end machines, high-speed connections, or a plethora of plug-ins. After all, the beauty of the Web is that it can communicate information to whichever user, with whatever device, at any speed.

Take a layered approach to adding features to your pages. Test your pages widely. A few powerful techniques will help your pages degrade gracefully and, with luck, keep those CEOs happy.

### Take from TV

Imagine if every show on TV began with the caveat "This broadcast is optimized for Sony twenty seven-inch Color Trinitron" or "Please buy a wide-screen TV to better view this program." Disruptive, inelegant, and ridiculous. So why do many Web sites greet their users with similar disclaimers? Telling visitors that they need to upgrade insults them. Either they will have upgraded before coming, or they will have a good reason why they can't or won't. Either way, it's not your responsibility to keep the Net community up-to-date on the latest browser developments. Your responsibility is to your creative ideas, so don't place barriers between them and large numbers of Web surfers.

One reason television works as a medium is that all shows work with all TVs (at least until we switch to digital TV). The Web can share the same advantage – if pages work with as many browsers as possible.

## The numbers game

A great way to line up your priorities for page degradability – and, perhaps more important, to decide the level at which you should pitch the heaviest version of your pages – is to do a little research.

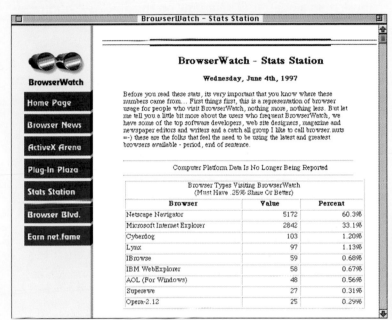

*Who Uses What?*

The browser wars are on, and the relative positioning of each client on each platform is crucial information for Web designers. If you don't have access to your server's logs, or you don't want to get that deep into the technical details of parsing huge log files, you can find help on the Web. Sites like BrowserWatch <www.browserwatch.com> and WebTrends <www.webtrends.com> keep a record of the browsers hitting their pages and then format that data for easy consumption.

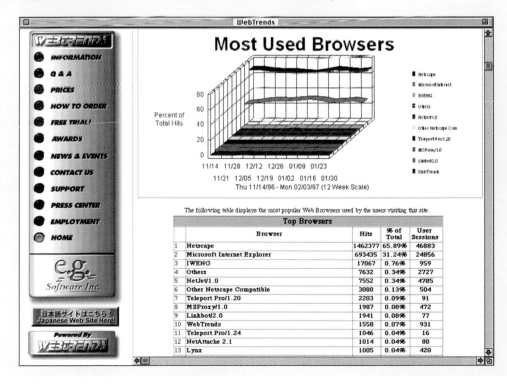

If you have access to server logs, you can crunch the numbers and see how your visitors' browsers stack up. If you don't have access to your own numbers, plenty of sites track these statistics in nauseating detail. A close look will show you where to put your efforts. If 75 percent of your users are surfing with a frame-capable browser, then don't spend more than a quarter of your time on the alternate nonframe version. Conversely, if only a third of your users have a Java-enabled client, then it may be foolish to spend weeks on applet development.

But maybe your stats reveal your site's limitations rather than an unskewed breakdown of users. If you have a graphics-heavy Web site with many layers of Netscape-only features, don't be surprised to see Lynx users bottom out in the lower percentiles. Your site drove these users away. So check another source for the Web's overall percentages of Lynx users and reconsider how to make your pages work for them.

*Who Sees What?*

**Tired of complaints from users who are not able to see your pages? You need to know which browsers support which features, but with the myriad of browsers available, it can be impossible to keep up. HotWired's Webmonkey offers a solution with the Browser Kit <www.webmonkey.com/browserkit/>. It's a database of popular Web technologies referenced to popular Web browsers and can help you make the hard decisions about what to support.**

Keep in mind that massive service providers like WebTV and America Online are probably grossly underestimated in your statistics because of their system of using proxy servers. AOL is the largest Internet service provider in the world, with more than six million users, and it's still growing. Doesn't it seem odd that its browser currently shows up with less than 5 percent of the market share?

This can be explained by how these providers dole out hits. With so many users fighting for resources on one system, AOL and WebTV use a proxy mechanism for speeding up their users' access times. When the first AOL user of the day accesses your pages, copies of your source files get saved on AOL's main servers, so when the next user tries to hit your pages, they get files from AOL's server, not yours. The proxy server occasionally checks to see if your pages have changed and downloads them again only if they have.

*The Browser Food Chain*

In the beginning, everyone pretty much just wrote her own WWW browser. Then again, in the beginning, everyone on the Web was an engineer. The rest of us eventually caught up and began aligning with our favorite method of accessing pages. The result is a legacy of assorted browsers, each with its own unique abilities and faults. Think of it as a food chain – small fish get eaten by bigger fish, which in turn are eaten by the biggest fish. Except, of course, as a designer on the Web, your pages should work with *all* fish.

**Lynx:** At the bottom of the chain, this first-generation browser is also the most basic one. Lynx is used as a last resort or when speed is at an absolute premium. No images are shown, and no distinction in typeface or type size is made. Everything just gets dumped to the screen as plain text – including forms. Recent advances in the browser are helping it to keep up (it can sort of deal with tables, for example), but for the most part, it's a dying breed.

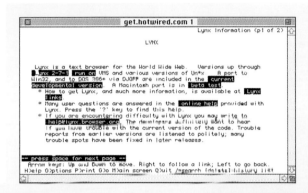

**Mosaic:** The first graphical browser, Mosaic brought the Web to the rest of us. Development of this second-generation browser has been slow recently, but it still serves as a valid way of surfing the Web. The most interesting thing about Mosaic is its history and nostalgia for the early days of design online.

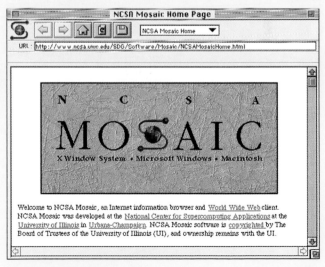

**AOL:** America Online's graphical browser used to be the bane of Web designers. It didn't do tables, it didn't do frames, and it was *soooooo* slow. AOL knew it too and eventually signed licensing deals with both Netscape and Microsoft, giving AOL subscribers a choice and getting the company out of the browser business – where it should never have been in the first place.

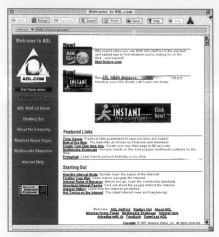

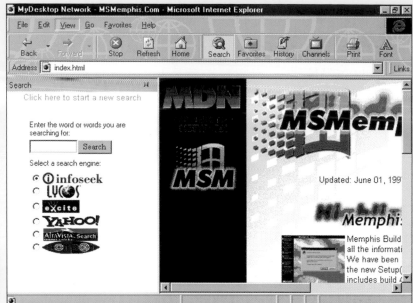

**Third-Generation Browsers:** Both Netscape and Microsoft are pretty much splitting the market now with their virtually identical offerings. Netscape's Navigator and Microsoft's Internet Explorer are the browsers that set the standards, and they are the ones on which most designers base their work. At this point, each browser supports most of what the other does, with a few notable exceptions like `<BLINK>` and `<MARQUEE>` (which don't really matter, since you shouldn't be using those dreadful hacks anyway).

**The Future:** We're starting to see the next generation of Web browsers now, offering true integration into your computer's operating system for seamless Web access, as well as things like dynamically changeable HTML and advanced style sheet control. Many of these features vary significantly from vendor to vendor, however, and it's still too early to know how all these new features will shake out.

These services are, in essence, keeping a local copy of the Web for their users, a practice known as caching. While this is an efficient use of network resources, it keeps AOL users from showing up in your logs. You can never guarantee the true numbers, so it's better to overestimate users of these services, which tend toward slow modem speeds and last year's browser features.

In general, err on the side of low-end users. You may see that only 4 in 100 visitors browse with Lynx, but again, that number is probably deceptive if you're looking for the percentage of your text-only users. All graphical browsers give users the choice of turning graphics off, and for users surfing through a 14.4- or 28.8-Kbps modem, that option is appealing after too many painfully slow image-laden home-pages. Most mainstream browsers will show the text alternative for an image (via the ALT attribute) if the graphics are turned off. Deciding not to support nongraphical browsers may save you time when putting a page together, but it's going to make your site impenetrable to a larger audience than you think.

An added benefit when you accommodate text-only browsers is that you'll be building *accessible* Web pages that can be used by people with disabilities. Degradable content can be read by a speech synthesizer, navigated by voice commands, or output to a braille device. It doesn't matter whether you consider this group part of your audience. U.S. census data estimates that 11 million Americans are visually impaired, for example, and accommodating them may be more than just a good idea. The Americans with Disabilities Act could very well change to include publishing – making it the law.

## The layered look

To make cutting-edge sites that still work for everyone else, conceptualize and build your pages as text documents that support layers of graphic and multimedia enhancements. At such a page's core is a basic text message that every browser can see. Images are the next layer on top of that message, then additional advanced layout capabilities positioning the two. Over that, add a layer of animation, then sound, then other multimedia. On top of that, carve the message into frames for navigation, or create a compound document architecture.

Using the proper code and consistent methods, these layers can be independent of one another, so that every browser shows the features the user's system can display but shows no sign of other missing elements. The result is a useful, complete page for every browser at every level. A Lynx user will know what your page says, but someone with a recent Internet Explorer upgrade sees how powerfully presented and entertaining the page is.

*Don't Advertise Plug-Ins*

Fright Zone's Halloween site <www.frighten.com> exploits cutting-edge technology, but it fails the user-experience test on the front page. Visitors to the site are required to know not only what version of their browser they are using but also what plug-ins are installed in their browser. If you don't have the appropriate software installed, the authors of the site conveniently provide links to the various software depositories, allowing you to surf from site to site, downloading and installing before finally getting past this front screen and into actual content. Assuming you had to upgrade your browser and download and install the appropriate plug-ins – all via a 28.8-Kbps modem – you would spend more than ninety minutes on setup before you could even check out the site.

This strategy may work in the CD-ROM world, where users routinely have to install software and restart their computer before using the title. But those users have made a significant commitment to the content (to the tune of 50 bucks or so) before even attempting to use it. The online world, in contrast, isn't accustomed to such barriers to entry. Why go through the hoops of software installation and long downloads when dozens of other free and easy-to-use sites are just a click away?

If Fright Zone's authors had made a layered site, they still could have served their cool effects to visitors who had the right configuration, without turning away everyone else at the frontdoor.

Good user interface is more than intuitive. It's invisible.

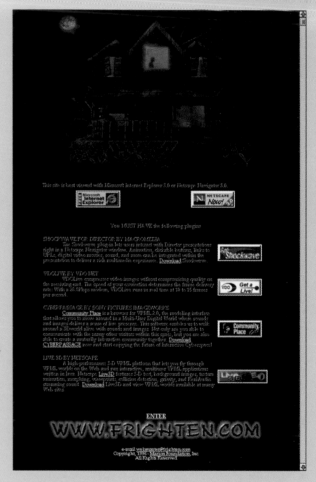

## No graphics? No problem!

Clever use of the simple ALT attribute of the `<IMG>` tag is a good first step toward layered pages. ALT attributes, which display text in place of graphics that aren't loaded, let you communicate the meaning of your graphical page to visitors who are using text-only browsers.

Well-written ALT text strings are like good headlines. They give a quick, clear description – and take skill and thought to compose. Although the rules for good ALT strings are mostly common sense, good ALT strings are not so common. For example, if you use a GIF for the headline "Massive Blender Sale", the ALT tag should say "Massive Blender Sale," not "Heading Graphic." That's thinking of your users' needs rather than your own. If the image serves as a link, use the ALT text to describe what the reader will find behind the link.

ALT attributes can also be used as a way to hide superfluous images from users who can't display them. Many page layouts before the age of absolute positioning and style sheets employed a stretched, one-pixel transparent GIF to push page elements around and attempt some sort of cohesive layout. That may be an efficient way to achieve those effects, but if you forget ALT attributes, a reader using a text-only browser would be left with a pageful of the default [IMAGE] indicators. As a rule, always use the ALT attribute, even if you leave it blank. ALT=" " will simply show nothing, as opposed to the visual garbage that leaving it out produces.

### Be redundant again and again

Making layered pages means building in redundancy.

Using a GIF animation? Older browsers will show just the first frame if they can't render the movement, so keep that in mind when designing the animation. Make your first frame an appealing one that works with the rest of the page.

If you are using Java, ActiveX, or plug-ins, you can nest HTML within the <APPLET>, <OBJECT>, or <EMBED> tag so that users whose browsers don't support the scripts or have the plug-ins will see a useful placeholder, rather than being reminded of what they can't see. For example, if you wanted to include a QuickTime movie on a page, this code could be used for anyone visiting your site:

```
<EMBED SRC="media/video.mov">
    <IMG SRC="media/snapshot.gif" ALT="A Dancing Bear">
</EMBED>
```

*The <OBJECT>ive Case*
<OBJECT>, <APP>, <EMBED>, <APPLET>? Don't these all sort of do the same thing? Yup. Each one of these tags incorporates some sort of media into your existing Web page, and each one does it in a slightly different way. There's a solution to all this nonsense on the horizon, however. The big browser companies are working with the World Wide Web Consortium on a standard way of achieving this, and they'll be settling soon on <OBJECT> as that standard. Eventually, you should be able to use <OBJECT> even to include other HTML documents in your page. If that makes your head spin, think about how frames work now: one document calls others into specified regions. <OBJECT> is actually a far more elegant way of accomplishing just that.

The <EMBED> tag brings the movie onto the page. However, browsers that don't understand <EMBED> will simply skip it and go to the next tag, which pulls in an image. Specifying ALT text for the image will give a description of the image (and movie) for those not able to view either. The HTML seamlessly degrades to accommodate all visitors to the page, regardless of their browser's technological sophistication. The use of these fallbacks is a powerful weapon in your design arsenal. It's the basis of intelligent, degradable Web content. Exploit it.

## The image map trap

Big, stand-alone image maps are the epitome of undegradable pages. Although both server-side and client-side maps allow you to specify ALT text, text-only users will not be able to find their way into your site. This is important, of course, when you consider that search engine robots – crucial for helping people find your pages – can't get into a Web site with an image map for a frontdoor. They don't see images, so they don't see your site. Consider using your own conditional HTML to serve a text menu in place of the image map for those who can't see graphics.

*Image Maps for All*

Image maps may not degrade as well as you would like, but the situation is getting better. Recent versions of Lynx, for example, now parse client-side image maps, turning them into selectable menus for text-only visitors to your site. This doesn't relieve you of your responsibility for creating easy-to-use navigational systems on your pages. Image maps should contain both client-side and server-side syntax to ensure the widest audience.

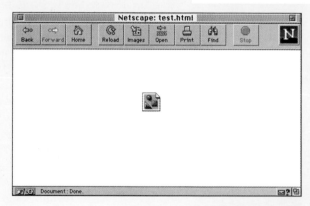

## Framing the issue

Building a site using frames should, in theory, allow you to publish to any browser. In practice, however, you will end up having multiple versions of your pages for frame-capable and non-frame-capable Web clients. HotWired's Cocktail section was designed specifically to exploit the navigational and structural benefits of a frame-based compound-document architecture. The technology of frames wasn't perfect – and still isn't – but we knew we could use basic frames to enhance our message.

Still, at the time we built the site, nearly 70 percent of our users were incapable of using frames. With this in mind, we designed the pages so they could stand alone, outside the frameset, and still present the weekly features.

Obviously, the site works better in frames, but we had the advantage of being able to build our content from scratch to work within this structure.

Using frames is just a taste of the feature disparity to come. As browsers evolve and become increasingly powerful, those left behind will experience an ever-widening gap in the seamless display of degradable content. Sure, adding ALT=" " to an image accommodated text-only users, and the <NOFRAMES> tag allowed us to simply offer an alternative version of our content. But consider a Web-based presentation making full use of dynamically changing HTML, absolute positioning, streaming video and audio, and the rest of the next-generation features springing up in the commercial browsers. Do we leave the last generation behind? Are we wasting precious time and energy by creating multiple versions of every piece of content we publish?

In the previous chapter, we saw that carefully separating highly structured content from its presentation and behavior was the foundation on which Web publishing was built. Couple that with the techniques and fallbacks in this chapter. The combination may be a utopian view of Web publishing, but it is an attainable goal: increasingly complex Web pages that intelligently map to the capabilities of the system on which they're displayed.

A good-looking page is only the beginning of the design process. You need to accommodate everyone. You need to reach for the ultimate in Web elegance. You need to degrade gracefully.

# Be Simple

No matter what you're publishing on the Web – whether it's an online version of *War and Peace* or a commerce site for your multinational megacorporation – your complex, rich, vast content must still stand up to the most sacred rule of Web design: Make it simple.

Creating simple Web pages requires clarity of message, elegance in design, and, paradoxically, code that can be quite complex. Writers, editors, illustrators, designers, and engineers must all bow to simplicity.

Take your clues from other forms of design – and specifically other media – while remaining true to the particular form of expression that is the Web. You need to place your designs in context for your visitors, using appropriate metaphors and avoiding the temptation to make things look "real." The result will bring success: simple and elegant pages and sites. But if readers must decode a page – if a design fails in simplicity and elegance – then you have lost them.

Above all, this responsibility belongs to you, as the interface designer. Though HTML may be easy, electronic publishing is a complex undertaking. But none of that complexity should be exposed to your audience. Work you fail to do will be left to your readers ... if they bother to stick around.

### Green means go

In trying to make Web sites cohesive little worlds unto themselves, Web designers often overlook their most valuable resource for simple communication with visitors: real-world knowledge. You don't have to invent a new visual language from scratch, because we already share thousands of symbols and systems. Green means go. Red means stop. The top of a page is the beginning; the bottom, the end. Big, bold words are more important than small print. You get the idea.

Think about this scenario. You're at the newsstand and you spot the headline "President Discovered to Be Foreign Spy" in red block letters on the cover of a colorful, tabloid-style weekly paper. You pay no attention. Then you see the same headline on a white-with-black-type newspaper with traditional daily newspaper typography and layout. Even if you weren't familiar with these two specific publications, their presentation tells you something about what their goals are, who their audiences are, and, ultimately, how seriously you should take the words you read on their covers. This cultural context is a powerful tool for simplicity in your Web pages.

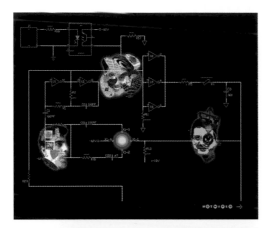

Over time, we've learned to pare down the visual clues that help move readers through HotWired's pages, by integrating signs and symbols from the universal set. For example, as our opening splash animation plays onscreen, introducing the site's feature of the day, our readers are presented with a tiny HotWired logo coupled with an arrow pointing off the screen to the right. Clicking on this logo brings users to the frontdoor. Placing the logo on the right and pointing with an arrow off the right side of the page, we call on our audience's ingrained knowledge of turning printed pages from right to left to move through a book. They know it goes to the next page, without our having to write "next" or "frontdoor" or anything else but the name of the site on the link. Likewise, an arrow pointing to the left would signal the ability to return to where you just came from.

*Salon* magazine <www.salonmag.com> has experimented with similar examples of idiomatic expressions for navigation. The convention of a dog-eared page instantly conveyed the idea of flipping through to more content.

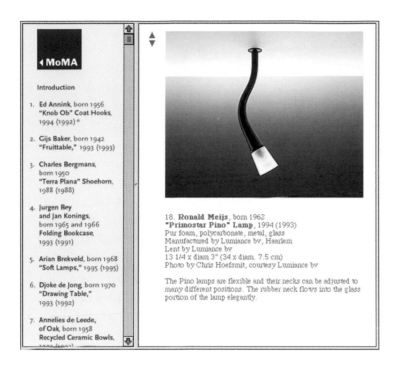

18. **Ronald Meijs**, born 1962
**"Primostar Pino" Lamp**, 1994 (1993)
Pur foam, polycarbonate, metal, glass
Manufactured by Lumiance bv, Haarlem
Lent by Lumiance bv
13 1/4 x diam 3" (34 x diam. 7.5 cm)
Photo by Chris Hoefsmit, courtesy Lumiance bv

The Pino lamps are flexible and their necks can be adjusted to
many different positions. The rubber neck flows into the glass
portion of the lamp elegantly.

For its part, the New York Museum of Modern Art uses a spare, self-explanatory system of navigation for its Web-based exhibit of Dutch Minimalists. While the frame-based layout allows users to click on any name to view the respective work, a simple combination of up and down arrows is provided as well, offering an immediately clear system of moving linearly through the content.

This all may seem obvious, but working dozens of contextual hints like this into your pages will let your readers focus on the experience of your content, not the interface that gets them there. Use what *they* know, and you won't have to teach them everything.

## Atmospheric conditions

As you weave cultural context into your site design, remember that consistency can give your site its own internal context. In a traditional publication, contextual clues are inherent, but they must be consciously put into place on a Web site. When you pick up a magazine, you immediately know how to use it. It has a front, a back, and a table of contents. You know how many pages it holds. Its physical presence is all the context you need. But on the Web, a homepage can be sitting at the top of a site with three pages or three thousand. And who's to say that someone didn't link straight into some random page in the middle of your site from a search engine or another site? The inherent physical contextual clues of print publication are gone; the online designer must provide the context.

Visual consistency is the key to fusing your Web pages into a single publication. The physical differences between *Interview* magazine and the *New Yorker*, for example, are immediately obvious – different binding, paper stock, ink, typography, and layout. All of these differences combine to form a frame of reference for every page of the magazine. So how do we develop even more context for our screen based designs?

The designers of HotWired grappled with how to make the site a conceptual unit from the first moments of this new medium. Bright, lurid colors and obtusely angled shapes identified all our pages when we launched in 1994. These choices distinguished us from the rest of the Web, with its default 23 percent gray backgrounds and bevel-edged buttons. With every click of the mouse, even novice Web surfers knew implicitly that they were still, in fact, at HotWired. While other sites would rely on large logos and navigational elements across the top of every page, we were able to subtract explicit elements from our layouts without obscuring our message. Using what came to be thought of as HotWired colors and shapes not only let us simplify our pages but also gave us a memorable visual identity.

Other sites have used an omnipresent table of contents to provide context and consistency across their pages. CNET <www.cnet.com>, for example, places a tightly integrated interface on every page within its domain. The yellow strip down the left side of the screen contains visual identity as well as a site map that follows visitors – this keeps visitors from getting lost, and it precludes brand confusion. But user convenience can come at the cost of variety and screen space. One CNET

**Customizing Colors – Past and Present**
Once our designers had defined the color palette for HotWired, we needed a simple way for applying those choices to our interface elements. At the time, our designers typically would create icons in Illustrator – which uses a print-based CMYK color scheme – and then export them to Photoshop 3.0, so they could be converted to the Web's RGB color scheme. Now, of course, almost all graphics applications are changing so as to accommodate the peculiarities of producing graphics for the Web. The following procedure, taken from an early HotWired process guide, shows the process we used to go through to apply custom colors with exact control.

We've typically been using the Mac version of Adobe Illustrator 5.0 to create icons and interface elements. Don't worry too much about colors; just get them close to what you have in mind. We'll be changing them in Photoshop anyway. The only other thing to worry about is text. Fonts render in strange ways in Photoshop, so before you finish working in Illustrator, change all the text to outlines by using the Create Outlines command in the Type menu. When finished, save the file as an Illustrator document.

Open the resulting Illustrator file in Photoshop 3.0. You'll be asked to enter the size and format. Look at the two check boxes at the bottom first. One will ask if you want this graphic anti-aliased (blended into the background, giving the illusion of higher resolution). The other box asks if you want constrained proportions (allowing you to maintain the height-to-width proportions if you resize the graphics). Make sure both are checked.

Now you can enter whatever you want to for the size. Make sure the mode is RGB Color. Click OK.

When the image has been rendered, convert it from RGB to

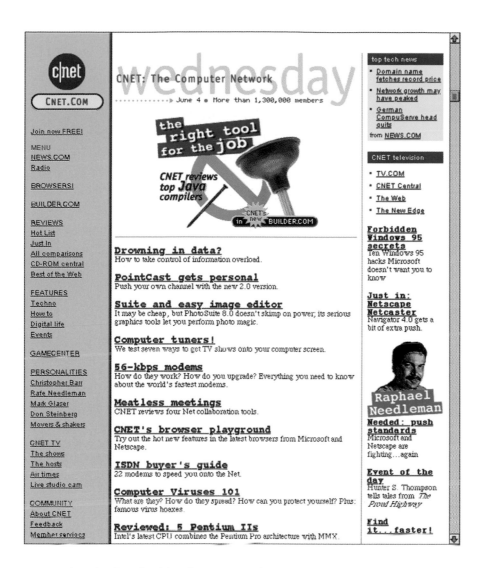

page often looks a lot like the next, and imagine a magazine using a full quarter of each page to repeat its table of contents.

Indexed Color in the Mode menu. You'll be asked if you want to flatten the layers. Click OK. Then you'll be confronted with a box asking you to select a palette. Choose "Custom...," which will bring up the Color Table box. Choose "Load..." and go find your custom palette. Click OK twice. The image is now in the right format.

If the Swatches palette is not already in view, then from the Window menu, pull down the Palettes sub-menu and select Show Swatches. When the Swatches palette appears, pull down the side menu, select "Load Swatches...," and again open up your custom palette. Now you can select colors from the palette to paint with.

Using the Magic Wand tool, select a color in the graphic that you want to change. Then select "Similar" from the Select menu. Now pick a color from the Swatches palette that you'd like to use, and select "Fill..." from the Edit menu. Click OK. Repeat for the rest of the colors in the graphic.

When you're finished, select "Save As..." from the File menu, change the Format Type to CompuServe GIF, and save with a new file name (ending in ".gif").

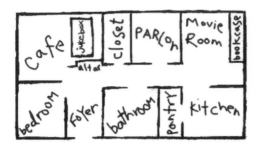

## Let metaphor be poetic, not literal

Metaphor takes the real world's system of subtle symbols and builds consistency into your site. Organizing a site around an extended metaphor is natural for designers trained in other media. Used well, metaphor can be a powerful way of letting readers know what to expect, of orienting them. For example, bianca's Smut Shack, <shack.bianca.com/shack/> plays on the metaphor of a clubhouse, with different rooms serving different purposes. When you're at the shack, you know where you are and how to get to the other rooms. Clear, familiar, simple.

*Southwest Airlines Home Gate*

*Reality Check*
Is painstakingly mimicking the real world a path to the best interface? Southwest Airlines <www.iflyswa.com> thought so. Assuming that Web users would be more comfortable with a metaphorical navigational scheme, the site designers created this airline service counter. To be honest, wouldn't reminding your visitors of standing in line at the airport be the *last* way you'd want to greet them?

But poor use of metaphor can have disastrous, embarrassing consequences. Designs become slaves to a conspicuous and unnatural reliance on visual reproductions of physical objects. A site can become trite and contrived. Basing a site design on metaphor may appeal to you as a shortcut – users quickly grasp the concepts being conveyed, because the concepts are being put in the context of

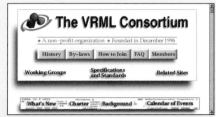

## Still Strolling, Not Scrolling

VRML, or virtual reality modeling language, has been talked about almost since the beginning of the Web. And it's a grand vision: users soaring through dozens of data points, swooping down to the day's news or banking over toward a reference library. It's a concept fostered long before the Internet existed. The idea was floated when the word *cyberspace* was coined back in the early eighties in William Gibson's sci-fi novel *Neuromancer*.

The reality today, however, is far from both Gibson's vision and that of the architects of VRML. Slow download times, poor desktop computer performance, and a long learning curve for good 3-D design have all conspired to ground this sexy technology in unending hype with little shipping code. Integration with current Web publishing has been difficult as well – virtual worlds may offer compelling navigational schemes, but actually reading an article in VRML has necessitated switching back and forth between the virtual world and a standard Web browser. Not exactly a seamless experience.

Still, there is optimism. The big players behind the Net have been pouring research and development money into VRML – most notably Silicon Graphics Inc. And the specification for describing these virtual worlds continues to evolve, if not at the insane clip of HTML. While you should avoid relying on this technology for now, keep an eye on its development. A simple, spatial way of visualizing data may, in fact, be just around the corner. For more info, see

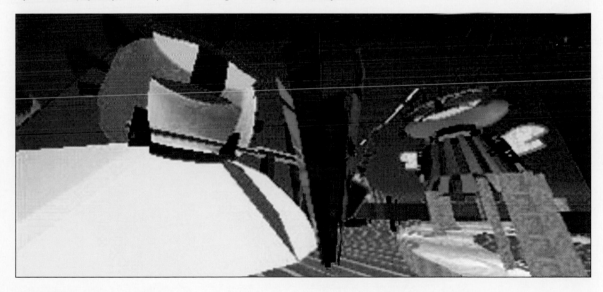

.

previous experiences. But if you continue to force page after page, element after element, into a metaphor, both the content and the user suffer the consequences. Ideas get sledgehammered into inappropriate containers, while users fail to gain even a superficial understanding of the underlying conceptual mapping.

This is painfully obvious with VRML. 3-D interfaces have as many pitfalls as forced metaphors do. Bad virtual reality is easy, but creating a natural, user-friendly interface in three dimensions is tremendously difficult. Must the end result accurately represent the real world? Do Web surfers really need to fly through a virtual information landscape? One of the Web's most compelling advantages over conventional media – the compression and eventual irrelevance of geography – is lost when you try to make your online world a 3-D model of the real world. You don't have to pass all the sites 'between" your site and another site on a server across the globe online, so don't artificially add that inconvenience to the Web, just to be like the real world.

*Learn from the Mac*
The book *Apple Macintosh Human Interface Guidelines* may be more than a decade old, but much can be gleaned from its pages. Not only does the work offer a firmly structured methodology for designing Macintosh applications, but it also digs into pure user interface theory and practice. User-centered design, cognitive mapping, usability testing, interface consistency, and more are covered in detail. And it's all online now. See <devworld.apple.com/dev/techsupport/insidemac/HIGuidlines/HIGuidelines-2.html>.

The designers of Apple's Macintosh user interface understood the power and the limits of metaphor. Mac users are presented with a familiar layout of a desktop, complete with documents and folders to keep them in. But where is the filing cabinet? Opening a folder reveals a window, not the insides of a folder. The designers of the Mac OS pushed their metaphor only as far as it actually helped their users. They could have created neatly rendered folders flying open, with three-dimensional documents being manipulated by representations of human hands. Instead, they created new conventions, avoiding exact physical representation and keeping things simple.

At all costs, avoid the mistake that manufacturers of cheap office furniture do when they put a wood-grain vinyl sticker over plastic. Don't make your pages ugly and artless in a quest to make them seem real. Does every navigational element need to look like a button, with shaded bevels to approximate depth and convey clickability? Why do objects need drop shadows, making them appear to float above the page? Designers cling to such cheap hacks – giving the *illusion* of reality – because of the immediate payoff. They can recognize the real-world equivalents and therefore feel comfortable using them on Web pages. But adding a bevel or shadow can be as cheap as using those wood-grain stickers. It denies the end product's integrity and ignores the simple beauty of RGB pixels on a screen.

Don't be a slave to metaphor. Use it wisely to simplify and clarify your pages.

**Simplicity is absolutely essential on the Web. As our network world grows increasingly complex, layers and streams of information constantly bombard us. Successful Web design takes control of content and boils its presentation down to essential elements in a subtle visual context. You can achieve this by using cultural, virtual, and metaphorical contexts to say much more than you can by writing long explanations for everything on your pages.**

**A careful mix of speed, technical prowess, and simplicity will make your designs more than just clear and understandable. It will enable you to push this new medium as far as it will go.**

# Being Obvious Online: "Click Here, Larry"

It was 1996 and Oracle CEO Larry Ellison was before a crowd of thousands, extolling the virtues of his pride and joy – the network computer. He gave a moving eulogy for Microsoft and Intel now that, in his most humble opinion, their era was fast approaching its end. The crowd waited patiently for the end of all this hyperbole, eagerly anticipating the point of his keynote address – a first look at an NC prototype.

Ellison finally moved to the small piece of hardware under the spotlight. He tapped a key and then logged into the system. Most of the techies in the audience were soon dismayed to learn that the whole system was simply a Java-enhanced Web browser with server-side email and calendar applets. In fact, when Ellison went to check his email, an HTML-based screen came up, replicating an in-box. The sender and subject lines were highlighted as if they were on any standard Web page – blue underlined text on a gray background. But the messages were numbered in the order in which they were received, and that number was at the front of each entry, set in bold. Ellison tried to open his first message, and as thousands looked on, he clicked and clicked that bold number *1*. Finally, after a number of uncomfortable seconds, someone near the front of the crowd yelled, "Click the blue words." He did, the message opened, and the crowd erupted in applause.

Ellison, being the head of one of the most successful high-tech corporations in the world, probably lost some credibility with the geeks in the crowd that day, but we shouldn't blame him entirely. Ellison wasn't a Web surfer and therefore didn't yet know rule one of Web literacy: Blue underline means click here. And without knowledge of that Net-specific sign, the design of the product told him that the big, bold number would lead to the contents of the message.

Those of us who have spent our careers online take for granted the emerging cultural context of the Web. Just as a magazine's pages are turned from right to left, our hyperlinks are underlined and our designs that are too big for a window get scroll bars. We count on people to know these idioms just as a city planner counts on citizens to understand traffic signals.

Yet a chunk of our audience doesn't have this grounding in online norms. New users, especially those new to computers as well as to the Web, often miss large chunks of content because they don't know they must scroll. Uninitiated surfers complain about icons that aren't obvious buttons.

Clearly, accompanying every hyperlink on a Web page with an instruction on how to click on and follow a link is overkill. Pages that repeatedly implore you to "click here" are victims of this atrocious instinct.

But for now, be careful. Shape your designs to match the level of your audience's sophistication. Pages built specifically for WebTV users probably shouldn't scroll. A Web-based card catalog in a public library needs to be much more explicit in its design than an artist's online portfolio.

As the Web's audience matures and digests its peculiar idioms, designers will be able to move on to other pressing issues. Eventually – for better or worse – scroll bars, blue links, and the obscure construction of URLs will become a universally shared language for our new medium.

# Be Fast

You spend hours creating your Web pages – optimizing each pixel, compressing down images to the bare minimum, excising every extraneous byte. In the end, you glow with pride over your lean, quickly transmitted, beautiful pages.

Take a stopwatch to the keyboard and reload your page. In the thirty-second range? Good, you beat the average.

Now look at television. A thirty-second advertising spot costs tens of thousands of dollars. Within that time, the creative folks at ad agencies can tell an entire story, communicate a complete message, change your mind, or stimulate your interest. Many are capable of doing that in just fifteen seconds. Back to your Web page. What does it accomplish in thirty seconds? It just gets the first pageful of images and text onto the screen.

Humbling, isn't it?

The rate of change in the computer industry is phenomenal, but bandwidth hasn't kept up. While processor speeds continue to soar, modem speed has only incrementally changed over the last decade. Many of us have 200-MHz Pentium computers, so why do we still surf at 33.6 Kbps?

Your job is to make your pages be *fast*. If you don't, people won't stick around to experience your work, no matter how rich or useful it is. Let speed shape every decision you make in Web design. Don't be left behind by short attention spans.

## A little more history: Net speed

When HotWired launched, we optimized the site for a network landscape that looks primitive from today's perspective. At that time, our studies showed that Net surfers' connection modes could be divided into three almost equal groups: T1 or faster (1.544 Mbps); ISDN (128 Kbps) and 56-Kbps connections; and modem users, who at the time surfed at 14.4 Kbps. Decisions on how to design graphics, lay out pages, and structure the entire site were based primarily on the speed at which our users surfed. We dreamed of a future with fat, high-bandwidth lines into every home, when we could serve every user the engaging, complex multimedia content we envisioned.

What we found, however, was that the ensuing popularization of the Net leapfrogged the technological evolution we had anticipated. Instead of a gradual rise in speed, we saw a sharp spike in the number of new users, all of whom were surfing with low-end modem connections. By the end of 1995, the proportions had shifted from the neat thirds of the previous year. Nearly 75 percent of our users were now surfing via 14.4-Kbps modems. While this bigger audience thrilled us, it doomed our high-bandwidth fantasies.

Since then, we've seen users upgrading to 28.8-Kbps and 33.6-Kbps modems, and with more corporations coming online, we see more T1 users. But the promise of high-speed connectivity at home via cable modems remains a dream. ISDN, still mired in telco bureaucracy and confounding setup procedures, remains a luxury for the technically sophisticated. In addition, millions of new users are taking the first few steps onto the Internet through America Online. Not only do these subscribers have to deal with slow modem connections and sluggish software, but they must also compete for resources on the service's taxed system.

The proliferation of Internet service providers has turned bandwidth into a commodity, but the technology still lags behind the demand. So, although we had hoped that the future would bring our users faster connections, what we have seen is a future bringing us *more* users with *slower* connections. So the task is clear: Fast pages or else.

*Prime Time Online*

You may not be the one responsible for the network behind your designs, but Net usage patterns are interesting to study regardless. Much like television audiences, Web users tend to flock to popular offerings with regularity. On the tube, the evening hours are considered prime time and are programmed accordingly. You would think online content, free of the linear stream of TV, would be significantly different, yet it really isn't. Watching daily network traffic, you see a small spike in the morning, as people grab their morning news. An even larger spike comes midday, as busy office workers surf a few sites during their lunch hour. The largest flood comes between 8 and 10 P.M., and that window of access moves across the United States as the time zones change. Prime time on TV and online are nearly the same.

What can you do with this information? Well, depending on your content and its frequency, you can create a posting schedule that accommodates your audience. We post the daily HotWired frontdoor, for example, after 9 P.M. Pacific time, knowing our greatest spike in traffic has just passed and ensuring fresh content for early risers on the East Coast.

Also, notice that during the prime time hours, you are competing against television. Drawing an audience away from the TV means that you must provide the same hooks in the same time frame. Yet another reason to design for speed.

## Big colors are fast

It's this simple: if you don't have fast images, you won't have fast pages. HTML tags and text are negligible in terms of file size – your images are what takes time to transfer. So design your graphics to be compact, and use the best compression format for different types of images. Skillfully wrought images will form a strong – and fast – foundation for your site.

Just two popular graphical file formats still remain on the Web – the same two that were available when the Web first took off. GIF and JPEG images, each suited for different applications online, are the building blocks of a graphical Web page.

A GIF (Graphic Interchange Format) image is compressed much in the way that Western civilization reads a page – from left to right, top to bottom. When you save an image as a GIF, your graphic editing application starts at the upper left pixel and moves to the right, then starts a new row at the left with the next pixel down, and continues down the image, looking for redundancy. If it finds many rows of pixels that share the exact same color, the compression algorithm will work well. Random or complex patterns of dots, however, won't get compressed. For this reason, GIF is more appropriate for icons and illustrations than for photorealistic images. Any image with solid, pure color areas will compress better with this format.

This may sound like esoteric computer science, but it's imperative to making an effective Web site. Design graphics for your pages that exploit this crucial feature of GIF images. Small graphic files mean quick pages that fit into the tiny attention spans of Web surfers.

*Understanding Compression*

You can design your images to have smaller file sizes – and thereby to load faster – by keeping the fundamental rule of GIF compression in mind when you design. Remember, the more color that is exactly the same in horizontal swatches, the smal-

ler the compressed image file will be in the end. For example, an image like this will shrink down to nearly nothing, as the redundancy of the horizontal strips of red and yellow gets encoded and compressed. Rotate the image, however, and the file size jumps. Each line of pixels must now be cut into several compressible chunks and therefore takes up more space in the file.

When Amsterdam-based artist Max Kisman illustrated HotWired's original icons, he used large blocks of simple colors to create the site's primitive signature. Whereas HotWired's print affiliate, *Wired* magazine, based its look on complex layering and visual blare, the Web site took the limitations of the GIF technology to inspire its style. A simple palette, combined with large, skewed shapes, created a visual language perfectly suited for the new medium – the images compressed well, loaded quickly, and stood apart from a cyberworld obsessed with rendered drop shadows and bevel-edged buttons.

On the other hand, JPEG (named for the Joint Photographic Experts Group) is a compression scheme optimized for photographic images. The amount of compression is variable – image editing applications allow you to choose the size of the file. The savings in kilobytes, however, comes at the cost of image quality. Whereas GIF images simply squeeze out redundancy, JPEG compression throws away pixels it thinks it can afford to lose. When you save a JPEG image, your graphics application asks you to set a compression level or quality level. You are, in effect, telling the program

*Precision JPEGs*
**Adobe Photoshop, for all its amazing graphical tools, doesn't give you very much control over the compression settings when saving JPEGs. Version 4.0 of the application gives you ten quality settings (which is six more than the last version).**

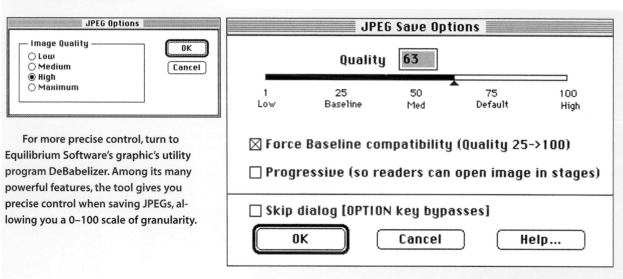

**For more precise control, turn to Equilibrium Software's graphic's utility program DeBabelizer. Among its many powerful features, the tool gives you precise control when saving JPEGs, allowing you a 0–100 scale of granularity.**

how many pixels must remain intact. The more you throw away, the smaller the file but the grainier the image. Experimentation is the key. Make image files as small as is acceptable to your design eye.

*Be Fast*

### It's not the size – it's the frequency

Mastering image compression is the first step in being fast. But the number of images on each page can bloat your transmission times as seriously as the size of the image files. The technology of Web servers plays an even greater role in the download speed of a page than the algorithms behind image compression.

Each time you include a graphic on a page, your server and your readers' browsers need to negotiate the transfer of that file, using the Hypertext Transfer Protocol (or HTTP, the familiar prefix to Web addresses). So, for a typical page, the following process takes place:

| Server: | Browser: |
|---------|----------|
| "I have one page with four graphics." | "Please give me the page." |
| "OK, here is the page." | "Please give me the first graphic." |
| "OK, here is the first graphic." | "Please give me the second graphic." |
| "OK, here is the second graphic. ..." | "Please give me the third graphic. ..." |

Not very efficient. The browser and the server go back and forth, asking for and sending and receiving each element on a page. In the Web's early days, browsers requested, downloaded, and displayed graphics in order, one at a time. When Netscape released the first version of its Navigator, the rules changed: multiple connections became allowable. Pages appeared to be displayed many times faster, because many images would start to render simultaneously.

An intelligent Web page, then, will have the fewest number of graphics possible, keeping the number of negotiations between server and client at a minimum and thereby speeding up a page. This strategy doesn't necessarily mean a reduction in the number of *images*, but it does mean a reduction in the number of *distinct graphic files* that must be sent. Grouping images well is the key.

A navigation bar that was used on Wired Source, our online research tool at <www.wiredsource.com> serves as a good example. Originally designed as individual images, the twenty-four buttons were later grouped into one toolbar. Not only did the files' overall size get smaller, but the page loaded an order of magnitude more quickly because it now needed only one HTTP transaction for all the graphics on the page.

The same was true for the lower portion of our search-engine query page <www.hotbot.com>. Although combining all the elements from the bottom of the HotBot page into one GIF made the overall file size larger, cutting out some ten connections resulted in a noticeable speed increase in loading the page. Remember that a GIF image with large blocks of solid color will compress very well. The long strips of transparent blank areas in this example squeezed down to almost nothing because of the horizontal redundancy of pixels. An early design incorporating a gradient blend between green and blue may have held more visual appeal, but it did so at a cost: much larger file size. The performance penalty was enough to spur a redesign.

Knowing your GIFs and JPEGs and understanding HTTP negotiations make it obvious that the worst possible design for a homepage (which *should* be a quick download) is the single large image map so often used by first-time designers. (HotWired's first homepage fell prey to that impulse.) Not only does a page like that fail to exploit any of the medium's unique capabilities, but it also leaves new visitors with nothing to do but watch the image load in the page. Conversely, blending text, which loads very quickly, with small and large images gives the illusion of a faster page, even if it takes more actual time to download. Visitors can start reading the text immediately, while images stream in and appear around the words. It's a subtle aspect of good technique – and one that is far too often overlooked by designers.

### Pyramid power

In theory, it's easier to get a million people to give you one dollar than to get one person to give you a million bucks. Same goes for site design. Getting unfamiliar

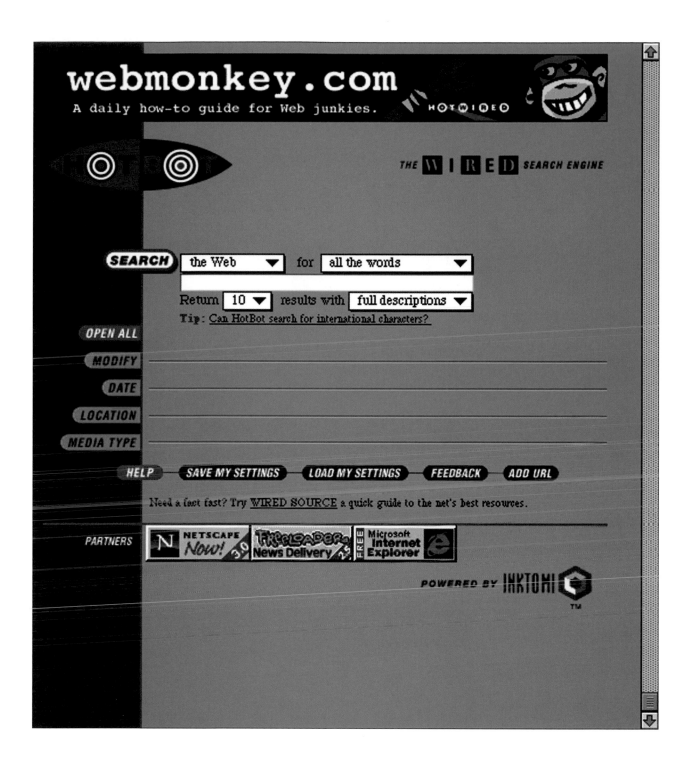

users to download a series of small pages is far easier than getting them to wait for one large one.

Picture your Web site as a pyramid shape, with one homepage at the top and widening rows of other pages cascading down, filling in an ever-broadening collection of content. A model for bandwidth usage can be overlaid atop that structure: Make the pages at the top small and the ones below them gradually bigger, until the final destination is the user's largest download.

Building up the bandwidth your pages demand as users get deeper into your site may at first seem illogical. Wouldn't you want to make the biggest splash right up front to hook potential readers? Unfortunately, the bandwidth you can afford to hog is a direct result of your readers' commitment to seeing what's coming. If they are forced to wait minutes just to get a page of choices, you will lose them. Instead, make the pages that preview your contents fast and sleek. Then, when readers have chosen what they want to see and they know what they're waiting for, you can serve them bigger, richer, slower-to-load pages, because they'll be willing to wait.

This means you need to compress your visual message at the top of your site. Small graphics, short and descriptive text, and sparing use of audio, video, and animations will make top-level pages pop onto the screen and will give a clean feel to what often can become a cluttered nightmare for users to navigate. Take an analogy from magazine publishing. How many different images and words does the typical publication use on its front cover to pull readers in? Choose simple and quick ideas to go with your simple and quick pages. Don't try to tell everyone everything all at once. People navigating the Web don't read; they jump from link to link, skimming from image to image. Their only objective is to get to the interesting bits of content you're hawking up front. Get out of the way and let them find it.

*Putting It All Together*
Create smaller graphic files, speed up the network protocols, and use fewer image files – a recipe for faster experiences on the Web. The World Wide Web Consortium has been putting some effort into researching ways in which a number of incremental improvements, when combined, can yield much faster surfing. Starting

NOTE-pipelining-970214

**Network Performance Effects of HTTP/1.1, CSS1, and PNG**

NOTE 14-February-1997

This version:
   http://www.w3.org/pub/WWW/TR/NOTE-pipelining-970213
   $Id: Pipeline.html,v 1.42 1997/02/14 21:54:19 frystyk Exp $
Latest version:
   http://www.w3.org/pub/WWW/TR/NOTE-pipelining
Authors:
   Henrik Frystyk Nielsen, W3C, <frystyk@w3.org>,
   Jim Gettys, Visiting Scientist, W3C, Digital Equipment Corporation, <jg@w3.org>,
   Anselm Baird-Smith, W3C, <abaird@w3.org>,
   Eric Prud'hommeaux, W3C, <eric@w3.org>,
   Håkon Wium Lie, W3C, <howcome@w3.org>,
   Chris Lilley, W3C, <chris@w3.org>

**Status of This Document**

This document is a NOTE made available by the W3 Consortium for discussion only. This indicates no endorsement of its content, nor that the Consortium has, is, or will be allocating any resources to the issues addressed by the NOTE. A list of current NOTEs can be found at: http://www.w3.org/pub/WWW/TR/

Since NOTEs are subject to frequent change, you are advised to reference the above URL, rather than the URLs for NOTEs themselves. The results contained in this note are preliminary - as we perform further experiments it will continue to evolve. When this work is complete and results considered by us to be "final", the status of this Note will be updated to reflect its completion. In particular, further experimentation with range requests is planned soon. Please check back again for further later results.

The results here are provided for community interest, though it has not been rigorously validated and should not alone be used to make commercial decisions. In addition, the exact results are obviously a function of the tests performed; your mileage will vary.

with version 1.1 of HTTP, a group of W3C researchers studied how the basic architecture of serving pages could be optimized. Next, they added the Portable Network Graphics format (PNG) to the equation – a highly compressible format that should be gaining popularity as new browsers begin to support it. And finally, they discussed how the power of style sheets could be used by designers to replace graphic files with plain text and formatting commands. The results are collected in "Network Performance Effects of HTTP/1.1, CSS1, and PNG," a report that can be read online at <www.w3.org/pub/WWW/Protocols/HTTP/Performance/Pipeline.html>.

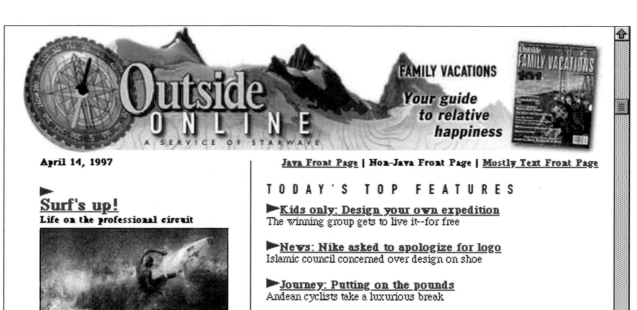

Outside Online <outside.starwave.com>, for example, offers users a quick path through its navigation scheme and into the actual stories. The frontdoor presents one large teaser paired with a few smaller, secondary teasers, all pointing to features deeper within the site. These links are followed by a pointer into a full table of contents – a collection of everything on the site. Rather than push everything to the user at once, the designers chose to present options in manageable – and *fast* – doses.

Providing shortcuts helps too. HotWired's fifth frontdoor gave our readers two ways to get to content that was interesting to them. They could follow the traditional route of navigation: frontdoor, click to section homepage, click to story. Or they could use the text blurbs on the frontdoor to jump straight into content. Two approaches for two types of readers. Our regular readers wanted to move through the hierarchy of navigation, looking for their favorite pieces of content and seeing what was new since they last browsed. Other readers, looking simply for an interesting new story had immediate access without the frustrating hide-and-seek game of navigating a large Web site.

Using these principles, you'll have two standards for file size and download speed for your pages: one for navigation pages and another for content. As you design your site, remember that readers aren't there for its navigation, no matter how brilliant. They will come for an entertaining or useful experience. It doesn't matter if your Web site is more a library or a gallery, whether you lean toward function or form. An unalphabetical dictionary wouldn't be a joy to use – it would frustrate and annoy its readers. And a gallery with the paintings hung facing the wall would be a waste of good art and good wall space. No matter how "serious" or "creative and intuitive" your message is, you still need to provide an easy way for readers to get to the stuff they want to see.

Look at a personal computer's desktop. As you open disks and folders, seeking for a file to open, little animations are taking place. Your cursor tells you when to wait and when to proceed, windows zoom open and closed, and files and folders are laid out in recognizable patterns and hierarchies. All of these navigational cues are part of the interface between you and your computer. They happen very rapidly – right at the edge of your perception, guiding you through a complex arrangement of information and allowing you to focus on the bits and pieces you need. But once you find what you're looking for, the experience changes from navigation to destination. Your work (or play or communication) fills the screen and becomes the only area of interest. You slow down and focus on the task before you. You spend more time once you get to work or play.

The same can be said about an effective Web site. Using fast graphics, fast pages, and inverted bandwidth, you can let your readers zoom through the top layers of your content and find their way quickly and efficiently to what interests them. Then, once they are in and have made the bandwidth commitment to your message, you can take a little more time to give them a seamless, vivid experience.

**In the end, it's another game of tug-of-war with the Web's capabilities. If you want to make eye-popping, resplendent pages, you have to know your compression, finesse your HTTP negotiations, structure your site intelligently, and inspire users' commitment. You can't be good without being fast.**

# Out of Simplicity
# Seize Your Style:
# Be Bold

Sit down on the floor with a deluxe 800-piece Lego SuperSet spread out around you. Take the flat green basepad and start building – a bunch of 2 x 6 blocks to outline the house you're building, 1 x 8 strips to frame the windows and doors. Stick a little LegoMan and LegoWoman on the little Lego porch, and admire your fine example of preschool architecture.

Feels like the Web, no?

Lego may seem a simplistic analogy for designing on the Web, but think about it: The tools you used as a child were easy to use, yet entirely compatible. If you had enough pieces, you could make whatever you wanted, but in the end it all pretty much looked like Lego. When you tired of simple building blocks, you could move on to more advanced kits like SpaceLego and UnderwaterLego. Of course, creative control didn't guarantee success: mixing Pirates of the High Seas Lego with Gas Station Lego just gave you junk.

Simple, bright, playful, full of contrast – the Web's aesthetic differentiates it from most other media, if not from children's toys. The design solutions of both Lego and the Web respond to limited bandwidth: children are in an early stage of mechanical and mental development, and the Web is saddled with slow transfer of information and primitive resolution.

Every piece of Lego fits with every other piece, just as every HTML document can be viewed on any computer in the world. However, you can't make 45-degree angles in Lego, and the chunky projects that result from building with Lego parts show that. Same too with HTML. In its purest form, HTML cannot control the simplest of graphic layout techniques; there is no face or font size selection, no margin control, and very little ability for placing objects in relation to one another. So the Web's visual building blocks don't make designing easy. You are going to have to use all your creativity and flexibility to exploit the very limitations that enable the Web to work as a medium.

You are trying to win the notice of a culture of insanely small attention spans, using a medium with trickling data rates and painfully slow displays. You must leave behind the world of slick, computer-generated imagery and high-resolution photos. The drop shadow and the beveled edge, the gleam of rendered light on an icon – these devices are dead. Smash your images flat. Make them by hand. Use a fat marker on a sheet of paper and scan it in and posterize it. Make symbols and pointers and icons blocky, simple, and useful in a matter of seconds. Exploit the beauty in bitmaps and the hipness of low-res photos.

Above all, be confident and daring with your visual language. Grab your readers. Snap them to attention, and throw them into your content. Don't look at your possibilities as primitive. Let them force you to be bold.

# Be Clear

You want a hip Web page, a cool site, killer content. Great. Just don't force your readers to decipher your navigation scheme to get to it.

According to HotBot, our search engine, today's Web is fast approaching 100 million individual pages. If you're going to compete in this ocean of electronic information, you can't confuse the people you're trying to reach. Your homepage is your storefront, your magazine cover, your movie trailer. Your content may be complex, elaborate, and intricate, but your navigation can't be. Get your best stuff right up front, make it brain-dead simple to grasp, and make it visible from across the street.

Think about it. Once a new reader has made it through the morass of the Web to your page, you have roughly ten seconds to make an impression, spark interest, and keep the cursor away from that Back button. Long-windedness, obscurity, and ambiguity are out of the question.

The solution is user-centered design. Don't let your readers get lost, but rather lead them down an unmistakable path through your content, based on a strong context and theme.

Look at each page through the audience's eyes. Offer users well-placed and skillfully constructed clues. Clearly orient them as they explore your site.

### Explain or explore?

Navigation is much more than pathways to content. Links through your site communicate your message, attitude, and ideas – whether or not you mean to. Strong word-and-picture pairs offer windows into the pages ahead, a portal through which a reader can view scattered content.

Once you figure out where your site falls on the library-gallery continuum, use that awareness to envision your site's navigation. Take control. Are you going to explicitly guide visitors into your content or let them intuitively explore? Are you going to do the work of explaining your site's organization or let your readers figure it out?

At HotWired, we jumped to another place in the range between *explanatory* and *exploratory* every time we redesigned. As we did, we learned that we weren't always being as clear as we thought we were. Our first frontdoor, for example, was bold visually but weak in communicating. We let visitors feast on unmistakably HotWired images and our hip-but-obscure channel names, but we made them do the work of decoding those symbols by going further into the site.

Compare the use of large icons representing general sections in the first HotWired homepage and our third iteration's pictorial teasers, which referred to specific feature stories within. The aesthetics remained consistent – strong colors with blocky and rakish shapes – but the newer design beat a clear conceptual path from the frontdoor to specific

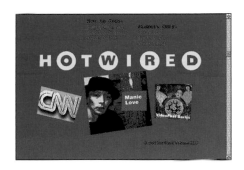

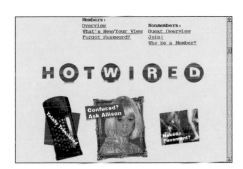

content. Now the site did the work, giving visitors more clues, more quickly, to what was on the site instead of simply presenting an array of mysterious choices for exploration. Featuring new content up front was clearer to our visitors than hiding it behind static section icons.

*Giving Clues with Client-Side Image Maps*
Client-side image maps on Web sites offer a great performance boost (server-side image maps require two round-trips between browser and server; client-side maps, just one), and they give users more feedback than previous technology allowed. Earlier, server-side maps required every pixel of the image to point to something, whether or not you wanted it to; with the default value of the maps set to point to the page itself, when a user clicked in an area not technically assigned a URL, the page reloaded. Not exactly the most elegant experience.

Client-side image maps have changed that. The map can be defined as having no default at all. When users pass their cursors over an image, the pointer can change from an arrow to a pointing finger informing them where they can click. A bonus: the destination URL is displayed in the window. (Server-side maps simply show the path to the image map program on the server.)

Know the difference: Client-side maps are faster and provide better context for your users. Server-side maps, while slower and less elegant, are far more compatible with older browsers. Thankfully, one image can support both types of image maps. Use them.

The channel list used in the fourth version of HotWired's front page gave readers a peek into the visual identity of our sections, as well as section names and a short description. But it failed the clarity test. Again we tested the tenuous balance between the obscure and the concrete – between eye candy and information – with varying success. Visitors familiar with our World Beat section and its cultural, travel-story focus may have accurately grasped its tag line, "The Rhythm of the Planet." But thousands of first-time visitors might have thought the phrase suggested coverage of world music. We failed to choose words that would work from a user's perspective. We were conceptually working from the content toward the reader, rather than from the reader toward the content. While this design explicitly showed people how the site was divided up, it failed to orient them to what was behind the range of choices.

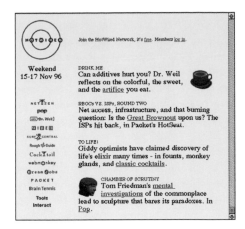

> IN COCKTAIL
> You like your family; you can't *stand* them. Nothing seems right during the holidays, save this undying concoction.

The next version of HotWired took an even more direct approach to bringing readers into the site: it combined icons lifted directly from the content with short paragraphs describing individual features, rather than the sections to which they belonged. It took the guesswork out of navigating the site. We could succinctly, but with some style, tell our readers what to expect when they clicked. Plain, simple, clear.

## Now or never: Don't wait for users to "get it"

Clarity need not fight with cutting-edge design. No matter how cool and hip your graphic sensibilities are, you cannot assume that visitors to your pages will eventually learn a confusing interface. There are dozens, if not hundreds or thousands, of Web sites just like yours, and they are just as easy to find. The sad truth is that if your readers experience any sort of confusion, if they feel lost in your hypertext, if they fail to see your metaphor, they will leave.

What would television be like if every show had a different remote control? Viewers would have to learn a completely new interface every half hour, and those interfaces would need to be as simple as possible just to keep users around long enough to learn new interfaces for the show's advertisements. Twelve-year-olds would love it, of course, and the geeks would proclaim the beauty of this open system. Truly committed viewers would watch the two or three shows they could find and comprehend. But most people simply wouldn't bother.

On today's Web, every site, every homepage, and nearly every piece of content on those millions of different pages assume that a Web user will stick around to learn their navigational peculiarities. If you can make your pages stand out – make your pages memorable and your interface invisibly simple – your readers will return for your content. If you don't, if you assume they'll figure it out, they will simply find somewhere else to go.

*Pointing with Pictures*
**With the fifth version of our frontdoor, we created a "river of text" that snaked down the page, flowing around icons. As time passed, we polled our readers and studied our server logs to see how effective the design was in driving traffic to our content. Not surprisingly, there was a general trend from top to bottom: content near the beginning of the page saw more traffic than pages linked below the scroll bar. Also, teasers paired with an icon always drove more click-throughs than paragraphs without. We learned a valuable lesson in clarity and communication. A tight coupling of words and pictures is more compelling to a surfing audience than links from the paragraphs alone.**

**User testing of the design before launch showed another common behavior. If a paragraph was paired with an icon, users always clicked the icon, regardless of whether the paragraph contained a text link or not. The most important visual relationships you build on Web pages are between words and pictures. Make absolutely sure your icons do their work: they draw readers in. Remember, people don't read Web pages – they skim them. Then they click on pictures.**

*Grouping Pages*

You can be only so clear through design –
your site must have a strong foundation.
If your site is a sprawling collection of
content, it must have an organizational
clarity that is immediate to your audience.

Many corporate Web sites group their pages within the divisions of the company –
administration, public relations, customer service, and so on. Other sites create their
own apt divisions: a mountain biking site may group pages by trails, gear reviews, and
hike recommendations.

Savvy Web developers, however, split the pages where
they make sense to their audience. Sun Microsystems, in
its online guide to user interface design and testing
<www.sun.com/sun-on-net/uidesign/>, recorded the title
of each of its Web pages on an index card and then gave sets
of the cards to test subjects. The subjects were asked to put
each card into piles with similar cards and then to name
each resulting pile. After the same exercise was conducted
on ten to twelve different users, trends
were easy to spot. The site was reorganized
according to patterns that may have been
difficult to spot by a design team too familiar with the content.

Think carefully about grouping your
pages. Step back and see your site the way
your audience will.

## Clear strategies

Explicit signals can guide a reader through content, explaining with each click the next appropriate step. But if style and
wit are more important on your site than practicality and
function, then make your site invite exploration. Either way,
you don't have to sacrifice clarity. If you can boil your
message down to something simple, compelling, and filled
with a powerful voice, you can mix information with exploration – and come up with brilliant combinations. Let's look
at some strategies that work.

**The Netizen** <www.hotwired.com/netizen/>: Devoted
to coverage of political and cultural
issues, The Netizen developed a style
the editors and designers referred to as
an "eyeful" of information. Each link was
presented as an elegant blend of a title,
an image, and a teaser made up of only

a few words. By paying as much attention to the individual pieces of the group as to their interaction, the editors developed a method of quick and effective linking that didn't spell out exactly what's behind the links but quickly gave enough bits of information to let people know whether the feature is of interest to them. Readers take in these units instantly, and traffic flows through the site as a result.

**BigBook** <www.bigbook.com>: A virtual Yellow Pages, BigBook knows the difference between designing a useful Web tool and a compelling Web experience. The typical BigBook user comes for information, for reference, for searching. He is not there for a work of art or entertainment. The design responds: simple pointers, clear typography, and an unimposing user interface. See how the most prominent words, *WHAT* and *WHERE*, are the ones that steer you toward the page's purpose – to find a specific type of business in your area. A bold, clear design, with little room for error.

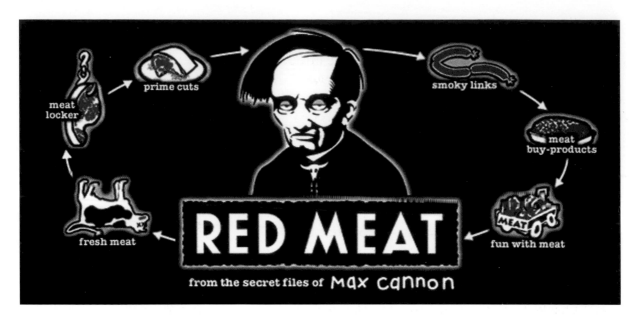

prime cuts

meat
locker

smoky links

meat
buy-products

fresh meat

fun with meat

RED MEAT

from the secret files of Max Cannon

## Submit to Style

Notice the search button on the BigBook homepage. When creating an HTML form, you have two options for getting the contents of that form to your server: the default button as defined by your user's operating system or an image. It works like this:

1. `<input type="submit">` yields the standard button.

```
Submit Query
```

2. `<input type="submit" value="Search!">` yields a standard button with your text.

```
Search!
```

3. `<input type="image" src="foo.gif">` uses foo.gif as a button.

```
Look It Up
```

**Red Meat** <www.redmeat.com>: The Web-based archive of Max Cannon's alternative comic strip pulls off a mix of wit, whim, and the Web. The site's designers have stripped away extraneous information, leaving only a strong visual language and a consistent metaphor. The "Fresh Meat" section points readers to the newest comic on the site, behind its intriguing dead-cow icon. "Meat Locker" is an archive, and "Meat Buy-Products" is where you can buy T-shirts and books. The site is indirect, yes, but not confusing or random. The metaphorical interface is instantly usable, stemming from such a clarity of presentation. Speed is of the essence, of course, in a site like this one, for without an immediate payoff for each click, reader interest will wane. The site also uses well-crafted, interactive mouse effects that do nothing to

BigBook opted for the image, and the effect is particularly successful. Not only does the button fit in tightly with the page's look and feel, but it can also be integrated into the design consistently. Had the designer used the standard operating system button, the element would have been different sizes from platform to platform and visually irregular. Instead, an image brings cohesion to the page and stability to the design – something to strive for in your own designs.

Unfortunately, clicking the graphical button generates no visual change in the button image. Platform-dependent buttons, since they are generated through code in the browser, give an indication that they've been clicked, either by inverting inform the reader but simply intensify the experience of clicking through an atmosphere of sarcasm and razor-sharp humor. It's the intelligent use of metaphor and spare but clear communication on Red Meat that let it get away with a style like this. The results are stunning.

Unfortunately, there are times when designers lose the line of communication with visitors and end up with a site that means nothing to the uninitiated. Here's an example.

**Pepsi Cola** <www.pepsi.com>: An early version of Pepsi Cola's massive site collapsed on its own attempt at hipness. Most notably, Pepsi wrongly assumed that attitude can substitute for navigation. Its sections were named "Concrete Box," "The Void," and other indecipherable titles, for which the illustrations offered no clue. Toolbars such as these give the hapless surfer no visual, conceptual, or mechanical clue as to what could possibly be lurking behind. On the Red Meat site, "Prime Cuts" could be nothing else but a collection of Cannon's best work. But what on earth did "Lava Lounge" mean in the context of a Web site about carbonated beverages? There was no context. Visitors were forced to learn an entirely new language with each click of the mouse. Why bother? This was a site that forgot that the people coming to use it didn't already know what was there – hadn't already cracked its code. On the path between exploratory and explanatory, the designers got horribly lost – and lost the reader with them.

### Boring ≠ clear

There are two dangers in aiming for clarity and directness, and you should constantly avoid slipping into either one of them. Don't overexplain, and don't mistake dullness for clarity.

colors or by visually appearing to depress. Through the use of JavaScript, BigBook's button could be given the same effect during a mouseDown event by swapping images during a click. Obviously, only users with recently upgraded browsers would see the effect, but that sort of attention to detail makes Web designs stand out.

Never stop experimenting with ways to make your site more visually appealing and user-friendly.

Being excessively elaborate about what's behind your homepage naturally leads to pages that are dumbed down to a lowest common denominator or weighted down with too much text. This can undermine your success just as much as obscurity. A store wouldn't think twice about putting an Open sign in the front window. But a sign reading "You can come In here and spend your money on stuff because we're all here now" defeats the purpose. The goal is to give readers what they need at the moment to orient themselves and make decisions – no more or less.

Be balanced. It's easy to err on the conservative side of interface and page design. Worrying too much about simplicity and clarity can lead to stagnant pages that never take chances. For example, user testing and focus groups can hamstring your creativity as a Web designer. Both are excellent gauges of your Web site's usability and accessibility, but only as an indication of success or a means of uncovering the show-stopping error. Don't let user testing become a design-by-committee process that leads to generic pages that offend no one and inspire no one. Use it as a guide – an error-checking mechanism.

*John Doe Blows It ... Over and Over*
Why is it that so many Web authors and designers feel the need to extend a personal greeting to each and every person who hits their page? Why not simply get right into the content or at least point to it with an effective navigation scheme?

Across the Web, from site to site, you'll encounter the dreaded "Welcome to..." greeting emblazened across the top of pages. The hospitality is admirable, but maybe this syndrome is symptomatic of a lack of anything to say. Please, just get to the point on your pages. We'll just assume you're glad to see us.

**The secret of clarity in Web design is to rigorously anticipate a user's process of discovery while eloquently and succinctly placing clues to your content in buttons, blurbs, and images across your site. Remember, your audience is not coming to your Web site to see the interface. Visitors want to see the content. Show them what you've got and how to get there. Then get out of the way.**

# Screens versus Streams: Think "Above the Fold"

The way we talk about the Web is largely borrowed from print. We say *Web publishing*, not *Web broadcasting*; we say *pages*, not *shows* or *screens*. But basic changes in thinking are required when moving from the printed page to a Web page. New-media designers first faced this transition in the early nineties when CD-ROM publishing was at its nexus. But the fundamental differences between CD-ROM and Web publishing are just as dramatic.

Very rarely do pages scroll down off the screen on CD-ROMs, whereas – for better or worse – they almost always do on the Web. Pages on the Web usually need the flexibility of an unlimited bottom, considering the variance in font sizes from platform to platform. Since the Web has no fixed page size, different computers will open browsers to different widths and heights, leaving the designer with only a general feeling of the areas of text and graphics on a page. CD-ROMs, on the other hand, strictly define the area in which the designer can work. Most multimedia presentations will choose a 640 x 480 resolution and black the rest of the screen, focusing users' attention.

Think of the two layout approaches as an opposition between composing screens and creating streams, or between static and dynamic layout.

Of course, the screen-based approach is possible on the Web, but it's fatally difficult. Resolution on a computer screen is terrible; most displays fall between 72 and 100 pixels per inch, a far cry from the 1200 pixels per inch or more in the print world. This limitation drastically reduces the amount of information that can fit on one screen without scrolling the page down. So in order to create pages within

*Gridlock*
**Discovery Channel Online <www.discovery.com> once used a strict grid system to create a screen-based layout. The designers could be assured that all users would see the same proportions, since all variables – such as white space and font size – had been cemented in place by using images exclusively. Even the features were originally based on the same screen size, making users click from page to page. Eventually, the designers moved their content into a stream-based format.**

a screen-based framework, designers must either create complex navigational systems for moving from one chunk of information to the next or rely on a simple, linear, page-to-page approach. Early Mac users remember the old HyperCard method of previous/next/home navigation, moving from card to card in a stack. Screen-based designs are almost always presented with a similar scheme.

**HOLY Smoke**
by Stephen Berg

I went to a small, religious liberal arts college. The fundamentalists who ran the place forbade many things—drinking, dancing, playing cards and smoking among them. Shortly before my freshman year I had gone through a powerful religious experience, after which I tended to agree with the local spiritual authorities on legalistic dos and don'ts.

So imagine my dismay when I walked through a friend's door and found him sitting in his dorm-room window smoking a cigarette. The smoke streaming from his nostrils was like the breath of Beelzebub to me. "Ferd, what are you doing?" I shouted. Lying on the desk by the window was half a pack of Marlboros.

I rushed across the room, grabbed the pack, crumpled it into a ball and tossed it out the window over Ferd's head. It was wonderful; I felt like I imagined Jesus must have felt when he drove the moneychangers from the Temple.

"What the fuck is your problem?" he asked. "I was gonna smoke those." He didn't speak to me for a week, and to this day remains mildly pissed off at me.

MORE

This was my introduction to the behavior of a smoker denied his illicit pleasure.

After many more fanatical antismoking tirades, my self-righteous actions eventually became as loathsome to me as they must have been to smokers and to God. In the Book of Isaiah I read: "All day long I have held My hands out to an obstinate people who say, 'Keep away; don't come near me, for I am too sacred for you!' Such people are a smoke in My nostrils, a fire that keeps burning all day."

Humbled, I vowed to hold my tongue in future encounters with smokers; as a result, I've learned the following things about them. The smoker knows he's killing himself. The smoker knows his habit is slowly bankrupting him. The smoker knows he smells like he's wearing Tobacco Fields #9 cologne by R.J. Reynolds. The smoker knows he's setting a bad example for his children, nieces and/or nephews.

But when anyone mentions any of these things to the smoker, he thinks, "Fuck you!" blows smoke in the buttinsky's face and contemptuously flicks ashes onto the floor. In fact, the smoker cares only when he coughs up phlegm into the bathroom sink each morning and wonders if he's really coughing up bits of lung.

I learned these things despite, or perhaps because of, my youthful religious convictions. You see, the holier-than-thou hypocrisy I saw daily in my "Christian" school led me to rebel. The most obvious symbol of my rebellion was to become a young punk who was going straight to hell with a cigarette wedged in the corner of his sneering mouth.

So I found a new religion—worshipping nicotine.

MORE

I've been a smoker for ten years, and for the first time in my life I understand what it means to "love the Lord your God with all your heart and with all your soul and with all your mind."

My demon of choice is Winston Lights Box. I like them because I've sat down once too often with a soft pack in my back pocket. Unfortunately,  I've found only a handful of newsstands in all of Manhattan that carry my brand in the crushproof box. So each trip out for some butts becomes my equivalent of the Moslem's pilgrimage to Mecca. Praise be to Allah, the Moslem's religion requires such a trip only once in a lifetime. My religion demands a daily trip to the shrine, no matter the weather.

After buying a pack, I open it and sniff the cigarettes. (They smell like raisins.) Then I put one in my mouth and pick up my Zippo, I feel the brushed steel against my fingers; hear the click when I flip open the lid; see the spark from spinning the wheel against the flint; then stare at the flame for a second.

 Each time I light a cigarette, I engage in this ritual; it's my own little holy communion. In my case, however, the elements are not bread and wine but a cigarette and coffee. This may sound like blasphemy, but you have to keep in mind that the word religion comes from a Latin word meaning "reverence."

By sucking mouthfuls of burning leaves deep into my lungs, I've developed a deep reverence for life. It's because I know that every drag I take brings me that much closer to death.

Each time I stub out a b[utt] in my overflowing asht[ray] I can say with the Psal[mist] "My days vanish like sm[oke]; my bones burn like glow[ing] embers.... I eat ashes [as] food and mingle my dri[nk] with tears."

Kw

Of the few successful screen-based Web sites, most use the technique only sparingly. *Word* <www.word.com> will often switch to click-through, screen-based layouts when presenting features but sticks with the scrolling, stream-based layouts for navigational section homepages. Its feature "Holy Smoke," for example, takes readers through a multipage journey of the joys of cigarette addiction.

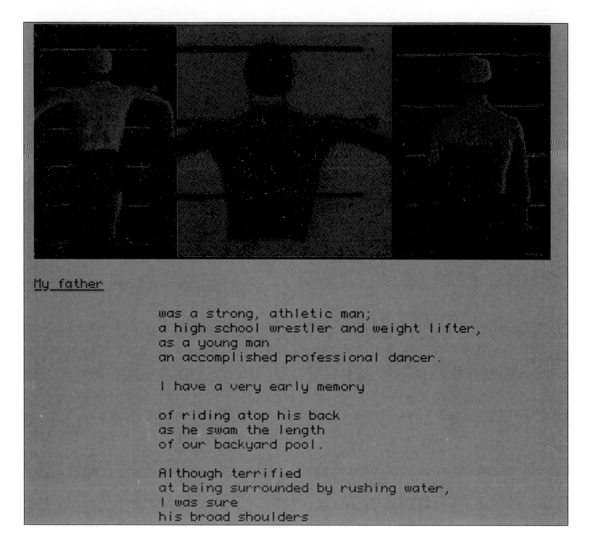

One of the earliest of examples of high design on the Web – Joseph Squier's 1994 creation, The Place <www.art.uiuc.edu/ludgate/> – made use of a static, screen-based design. In his piece "Life with Father," Squier used simple graphics and preformatted text to make the most of the very limited state of HTML at the time. But by spreading the work over dozens of pages and linking those pages in a sequential order, he precisely paced the unfolding story. The graphics evolving from page to page complemented the increasing intensity of the story, drawing readers in and holding them from click to click.

Scrolling layouts are far more common online, mostly because maintaining a single document is far easier than managing a cluster of linked pages. However, a number of problems remain inherent in streaming pages.

Many Web site designers simply create pages based on the design at hand, not realizing that visitors are moving from page to page and are being forced to resize their browser window with each click. Define a size for all of your pages, and never exceed it. Based on an industry-standard of 640 x 480 screen resolution, and taking into account browser interfaces and screen real estate, a width of 500 to 550 pixels is safe. And please, just assume your readers will understand this. Don't tell every visitor to resize the browser window.

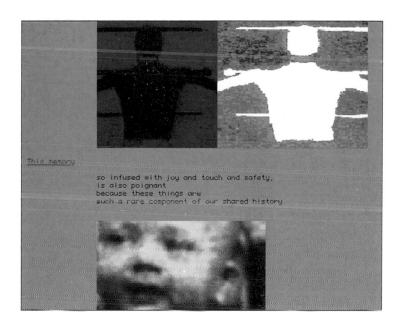

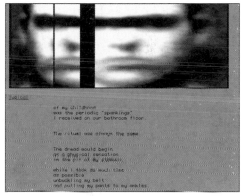

Despite growing sales in "multimedia-capable" computers, a big contingent of users still stare at measly thirteen-to-fifteen-inch monitors. Such displays can show only the first five or six inches of a long, scrolling Web page.

So the top of your page should be treated in the way that newspapers treat their front page "above the fold." This is where visitors are introduced to the content and where they will decide whether to dig deeper. Many sites fill the top of the page with interface elements – advertisements, navigation devices, section headers, and large titles – leaving no room for content. The designers of such pages are typically blessed with twenty-inch monitors. Simplicity demands a clear message immediately, and the top of the page is the only place you have to accomplish this.

# Subvert Hierarchy

Back in the summer of 1995, two guys from HotWired's production team decided to tell the world what they thought of the nascent Web. They wrote a rant every day and then made that rant the center, the opener, and the sole attraction of a Web site so simple it revolutionized navigation design. When you pointed your browser to their project, at <www.suck.com>, you immediately found yourself reading that day's acerbic, funny column, requiring nothing more to click or choose.

At the time, this was pretty radical stuff. Without fail, the frontdoor of every other site on the Web was a list of choices and paths to other lists of options, with actual content buried away from sight. And usually it took a good memory and careful reading to figure out what was different since you'd last been there.

The Sucksters gave people one thing to read, right now. No navigation. No cognitive map for a visitor to develop. It worked. Readers came back, every day.

# Suck.

*"a fish, a barrel, and a smoking gun"*
for 28 August 1995. *Updated every* WEEKDAY.

## *Live Through This*

There's something exciting about
the breaking of news on the Web
that can make an otherwise
bullshit-quality story smell
sweeter than Glade
Potpourri-in-a-Spray. Whether
it's two zillion critiques of a
<u>handicapped Time cover feature</u>

---

Two lessons from *Suck's* deceptively simple site design will make any site vital and dynamic, especially a site with frequent new content: Don't make people guess what's new – promote it, display it, lead with it. And, don't let your front page hide your content – make it the content in itself.

### No nesting

When you learned to use a computer, you learned to think hierarchically. Since the beginning of the personal computer, work has been organized in files that are nested into folders, all on a hard drive or network. Files and directories are structured in a vast tree, with branches leading down into the depths of an organizational structure.

This is undoubtedly how you will structure the back end of your Web site. Whether it lives on a Macintosh running a personal server or on an array of UltraSparcs pumping out millions of hits a day, nesting files and folders is often the best way of organizing a production system for your content.

But when it comes to presenting your site to your audience, forget the tree. Your file structure and what the visitor experiences as a site structure can and should be completely independent of one another.

Conceptually, this can be a hard leap to make. First, stop thinking of your top-level page as a static document. True, there is one index.html that sits at the very top of all the other pages on your site. It is the document everyone will see first when they go to your URL. But it doesn't have to exist as a simple menu listing everything else. Make it a window into your site – and a place to start experiencing your site's content immediately.

## Time, the final frontier

When you publish on the Web, you throw out the third dimension. Navigation on the Web works from any point to any point and isn't bound by distance or proximity. But, at the same time, you start to work in another dimension that your print publishing or multimedia production background doesn't prepare you for – time. Imagine your site moving through time, organized by the moment a visitor arrives rather than by the subjects you have to offer.

When you shift from subject-based to time-based divisions of content, your pages come alive. Replace your static menu with an automatically updated list of what's new – or combine that with starting one of your newest features on your frontdoor. Make it so visitors have no reason to hunt for the most relevant information. Make it so they just can't miss it.

In the evolution of HotWired's frontdoor, we started with the basic hierarchy, those simple static pointers to our five channels. Over time, we modified them, adding more-dynamic teasers to particular features. But it wasn't until the fifth iteration that we began to work in the dimension of time, making the site reflect the content's newness by reinventing itself every day.

In developing the daily HotWired, we created a frontdoor that would accurately reflect what a frequent visitor needed to know *right now* about what was new on the site. We deemphasized the conceptual structure of HotWired – the programs inside channels inside a Web site. That treelike structure was still there (just as it exists in our Unix file system), but our readers no longer needed to climb the trunk, because they could jump to what was new in each section directly from the frontdoor. We flattened the interface and painted a picture of what HotWired was that day – a window moving through time.

But perhaps the biggest change was the shift to a daily animated splash. In a spin on the *Suck* principle of starting to tell your story as soon as a visitor arrives, each day we made a little animated narrative inviting people into one piece of new content. This splash was the first thing a surfer encountered when hitting <www.hotwired.com>. It not only set the stage for a chosen piece of content for the day but also gave our readers something fun and surprising to expect on a daily basis.

We added visual clues to tell our readers that they were looking at a changing page. We dated each frontdoor and used the background color of the page to map the day of the week: Monday was red, Tuesday blue, Wednesday green, and so on, further ingraining the daily nature of the page.

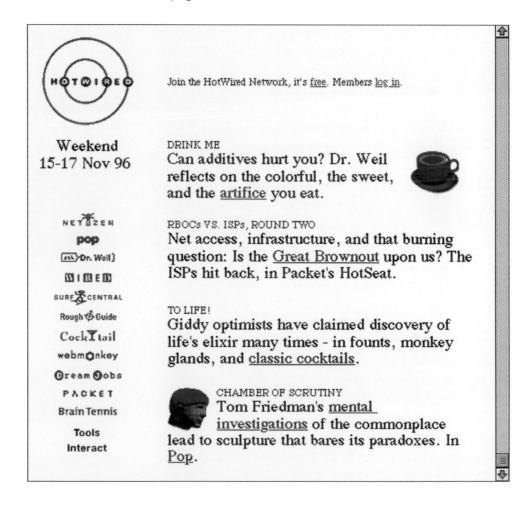

## The daily grind

Typically, our brilliant solution unearthed new problems. We were producing far more content than *Suck*'s essay-a-day format, so we needed both internal site structure and daily fluidity. We needed to convey both the ephemeral (new features) and the permanent (site organization) on HotWired. While our readers traveled through time, we had to orient them in the space of the site as well.

The information on our homepage began to simultaneously show the rigid structure of our site and the fluid daily history we were creating. Directly below the date stamp, our visitors could find a list of the site's basic sections. Visitors familiar with our content were offered a direct path to their favorite destinations; they could navigate without browsing.

The meat of the page, however, consisted of blurbs of text produced daily as teasers into fresh content. Written with the immediacy of newspaper headlines and often tightly coupled with compelling visual iconography, the teasers gave context for new or occasional surfers – by far the most prevalent subset of Net users.

HotWired isn't the only Web site trying to balance a space-time continuum through content and navigation. *Salon* <www.salonmag.com> offers its readers similar options for accessing its content. Each day, the site presents a new window into content – a magazine cover of sorts – that highlights a new feature. A sidebar points to other, smaller changes to the pages, such as a new post to its Media Circus section or a recipe addition to the Surreal Gourmet department. *Salon* offers two views of its archive,

**MOVIES:** "Volcano" | "All Over me" | "Romy and Michele's High School Reunion"

TABLE TALK  COLUMNISTS  21ST  TASTE  WANDERLUST  GAMES  COMICS  CONTACT US  ARCHIVES

as well – one grouped by date, the other by subject. Visitors can read articles in chronological order or explore different areas of interest. It's an effective way of acting as a library *and* a window through time.

### The past revisited

On our daily HotWired frontdoor, visitors could easily move through present content, but how could they jump off the level of the present and explore the history of our content back through time?

The interface for our archives closely reflects our frontdoor in structure, utility, and appearance. A list of content areas along the side of the screen again acts as a map, but this time into the individual archives of our network's channels. These individual archive pages offer readers the chance to

*What's the Frequency?*

Why the push for daily content? Quite simply, the purpose is to build a relationship with your audience that doesn't fade over time. With the constant bombardment of information hitting people from all media, you need to create a habit in your readers. Make them come back every day, even if your content isn't pushed out that often.

Most publications in the print world follow a set schedule based solely on printing restrictions that are intimately tied to their content. Newspapers print continuously, updating as fast as events occur and creating a disposable product. A monthly magazine takes longer to collect, design, and edit its material, presenting it in a more "valuable" package.

These restrictions are eliminated on the Web. You can publish whenever you like, since the printing, binding, and shipping process isn't an issue. Many publishers online have exploited this liberation by taking their content, however deep and involved, and trickling it out daily.

Don't box yourself in with holdovers from the mechanical age. Combine automation and a flexible schedule to push information out all the time. On the Web, immediacy reigns.

Surfing as jeff. Change your preferences?

## Archives

Packet
Flux
Markets
Tech
Culture
HotSeat
Media

Webmonkey
Browsers
Plug-ins
HTML
Geek Talk
Demo
Net Surf

**FRIDAY, 25 APR 1997**
bianca's core trolls hold forth in Packet's HotSeat, Webmonkey harshes on WYSIWYG HTML editors, and Cocktail presents the Scofflaw. (splash)

**THURSDAY, 24 APR 1997**
Packet examines Microsoft's dance with the counterculture, Webmonkey teaches you to roll your own search engine, and Dream Jobs trips out on the Experience Music Project. (splash)

**WEDNESDAY, 23 APR 1997**
Webmonkey tells you how to code your own search engine, Packet tracks the migration of the browser from desktop to handheld, and Katz has the *really true story* of that missing A-10 aircraft. (splash)

browse through all the past articles in a chronological order, and that option is presented consistently across all channels.

The rest of the page offers a day-by-day historical account of our frontdoor content, highlighting the important events and features of the past. This account trails back a couple of weeks, but an interface at the bottom opens up the entire daily history of HotWired, either in monthly chunks or, despite its unwieldy mass, the whole works at once. Giving users control of the temporal window – the ability to slide back and forth through history – is a benefit unique to Web publishing. Only through the Web can publishers offer the speed, depth, *and* breadth of a comprehensive, easily accessible archive. It's like publishing a magazine and knowing that none of your readers will ever throw a copy away.

**Using these two techniques – placing actual content at the top of your site structure and making your frontdoor change through time to match the pace of your content – will give visitors a sense that they're missing out if they don't come back to your site often. And when they do come back, they'll find a compelling experience from the first moment, instead of two or three clicks in.**

# Splashing Down: How We Mastered Mini-Movies

When we liberated HotWired from a static hierarchical site structure, we felt a sudden creative freedom that led to one of our biggest breakthroughs: frontdoor splashes. The short, entertaining animations that welcomed visitors to the site and promoted one of our new features were simply a clever use of a common technology. They have become our most imitated idea.

These little movies, almost comic strips brought to life, were created as small, quickly transmitted animated GIF images. We took inspiration from MTV's groundbreaking use of short station IDs to give their whole channel attitude, style, and coherence. The difference was that splashes carried a message rather than straight branding.

The editors and designers on the splash team learned fast that short GIF animations made the work on the rest of the Web look flexible and easy. Web design rules of simplicity and clarity became, for them, commandments.

*Subvert Hierarchy*

For example, since users accessed HotWired with modems as slow as 14.4 Kbps, and since each splash was a necessary gateway to the rest of the site, the final file size couldn't be any more than a tiny 50K. This, for designers, necessitated an exercise in self-discipline. They had a tiny area to work with (generally only 220 x 190 pixels), they had to keep the number of colors in each splash's palette to a minimum, and they learned to make clever pacing take the place of elaborate motion. Suddenly, the pauses between frames took on increased meaning. The designers used juxtaposition of images, blurred transitions indicating speed, and subtle visual clues to make up for the format's weaknesses.

The rigor of producing these little creative bursts five days a week for more than a year ensured that the results ranged from odd near-misses to glimpses of brilliance. But like all of Web work, each one was a testament to discovering what's possible within the boundaries of rigid technology. To see some of these splashes from the past, visit <www.hotwired.com/frontdoor/archive/>.

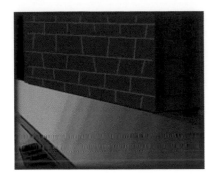  

Thank God it's over.    Thank God it's over.    Thank God it's over.    Thank God it's over.    Thank God it's over.

Attacks on servers are no joke!

Thank God it's over.

Thank God it's over.

Thank God it's over.

Thank God it's over.

# Master Hypertext

Before there was content, there was the link.

At the dawn of the Web's history, way back in the early 1990s, most Web pages were little more than vast lists of links to other pages. "Surfing" the Web and using a "browser" became part of our vocabulary for that reason. Nobody read anything – they merely jumped from link to link to link, looking in vain for something interesting.

Remember your first homepage? A grainy scan of your driver's license photo, a paragraph about who you were, and then links to everyone you knew and everything you thought was cool? In this democratic medium, where everyone could publish, we soon realized we had nothing to say. We substituted pointers – links – for ideas.

Be careful with hypertext. Those little blue scars scattered on today's Web pages wield an amazing power but are dangerous in the hands of the inexperienced designer. They are a visual challenge, filling carefully designed pages with clutter and distraction, pulling at your reader's attention. And without even realizing it, you're leading people away from your site after you've worked so hard to get them there.

Effective linking comes from clear design plans. It takes both visual and editorial skills, with a bit of programming as well. You must take a smart, multidisciplinary approach to hypertext if you want to make your site more potent, rather than simply offering your visitors a way out.

Hypertext is more than just a powerful tool; it is also an art. Taking control of hypertext will make your content strong, your design clear, your site fast, and your navigation simple – a recipe for success.

### Don't interrupt

In other media, navigation doesn't have to coexist with content. Television tempts you with images and prompts you to stay up for "News at 11," but it doesn't list other channels or options as you're watching a show. Newspapers and magazines offer a table of contents to draw readers deeper into their pages. But once you're on a page, you don't get constant reminders of how to leave and where else you can go.

On the Web, however, navigational signals don't stop once you get to content. They are peppered throughout. Not only does a Web site offer you a way to move through its own pages, but the actual words you read may offer link after link of alternative paths to other sites. Rampant hypertext can make your pages a dizzying mishmash of options, leaving your readers unable to focus on *your* content.

Think about how our minds help us make sense of the world we see. We're constantly bombarded with visual information; we can't possibly deal with every bit that passes through our eyes. To cope with this overload of data, we unconsciously group nearly everything we see into patterns: leaves group into branches, which form trees, which make up a forest. Without this ability, we would stumble through the world, trying desperately to remember and comprehend each individual leaf. We control the overwhelming visual clutter by reducing it to manageable sets.

The same is true on a page. Individual words combine into sentences, grouped into paragraphs, collected into a body of text. Carefully arranging the individual elements of a page into recognizable patterns gives a designer the leeway to imbue meaning to the whole. And by carefully breaking that pattern, with color or typography or placement, you can focus a reader's attention on the most important elements. A headline, for example, is larger and heavier than the body text – it jumps out of its surroundings because it is made to be read first.

Unfortunately, hypertext on the Web has the same effect as headlines, albeit unintentional. Links interrupt the visual patterns that make text work. Try reading a sentence with a link in it without being pulled away from the ideas being expressed. If you were reading this on the Web, the preceding sentence not only told you that a hypertext link was available under the blue word *link* but also forced you to decide whether you should follow it. Look at this paragraph as a whole. The word *link* stands out above all others. It pops out of the words around it, drawing attention to itself and stopping you both visually and conceptually.

We all fall into a rhythm when we read. Words and phrases flow together as our eyes move through a paragraph. Patterns form, and we escape the mechanics of reading. But the visual impact of a link is like talking with someone who occasionally breaks out of a normal tone of voice to shout one word or phrase. The flow is broken; the mind starts to wander. Coming across a glaring spelling error in a published work has the same effect: Your sense of suspended reality is lost. You are no longer in an author-created world – you are merely sitting with a book.

**Margins and errors**

Inevitably, first-time creators of Web pages make the same hypertext mistakes: sloppy, distracting, undisciplined, indiscriminate linking. But these problems are universal, and talented designers are continuously searching for solutions. We can look to them for a glimpse into the experimental process of solving the hypertext dilemma.

Feed <www.feedmag.com>: With a history of effective design and smart online publishing, *Feed* features an uninterrupted flow of text down the page; links are never added to paragraphs. Instead, they are moved to the margins and given context by tagging them with a colored, pre-defined label. The Commerce heading, for example, has

# The Thinkers

## Austin Bunn on Washington's conservative brain trust

*"In 1975, we used to say a phone booth was just about big enough to hold a meeting of conservative intellectuals in Washington... We were considered irrelevant by opinion makers in the media and the power brokers in Congress ignored us. They said 'conservative think tank' was a contradiction in terms. Conservatives have no ideas. History, of course, has proven them wrong."*

-- Statement from the Heritage Foundation, 1985

It is the kind of room only your father would be comfortable in. Middle-aged men in suits peer at the portrait of Ayn Rand and the copy of "The Wealth of Nations" enshrined in a glass case. A quick assessment of the 150-person crowd reveals the predictable minority count: 1, but even he looks jumpy at 8:30 am. Women: about 6 and dwindling fast. With the sole exception of the Mexicans in tuxedos rapidly clearing the breakfast buffet, the only local color here is navy blue.

It may be hard to believe, but these men are attempting to decide the future of the Internet. Harder still is the fact that they just might. At the conference entitled "Regulation or Private Ordering?" hosted by the Cato Institute in Washington, scholars, law professors, and the odd public servant (Lori Fena from the Electronic Freedom Foundation, the lone female panelist) discuss everything from the recent controversy over P-Trak to the contractual validity of marriages on IRC. What's most surprising is not how broad the conference is but how specific. These PhDs and public intellectuals are talking about TCP/IP and 'NetNanny' with startling precision. You're half expecting someone to start a multimedia demonstration until someone does.

**"None of us is smarter than the 200 million people operating in the marketplace," says David Boaz.**

Though the conference is framed as a "panel" discussion, the audience nods along while the speakers keep coming to same conclusion: deregulation. In fact, the agreement among the scholars is exactly the point of the conference and the institution itself. The libertarian Cato Institute, joined by the ultra-conservative Heritage Foundation (ex-Education Secretary William Bennett's stronghold) and the American Enterprise Institute (home of Charles Murray and Dinesh D'Souza), have come to steer the legislative process in Washington, by thinking more about these issues than anyone else and hammering away consistently at the same point. It's a trick that the handful of liberal tanks haven't tried. Underfunded and less organized, The Brookings Institution and the Institute for Policy Studies are fighting internal battles while the conservatives are fighting the real war. Liberal think tanks can't match the towering signal-to-noise ratio of the Cato because they allow too much on the dial.

With the support of billionaire financiers and a plethora of foundations, this conservative brain trust now acts like a legislative free agent: a nimble "power elite" of experts responsible for shaping policy but accountable to no one. Congressional staffers view Cato and Heritage scholars as the key architects of the major policy reform of the year -- ending welfare -- but to the general public, these architects are faceless. While the shady dealings of political consultants has been dragged into the spotlight -- most recently by the Dick Morris affair -- think tanks still elude public scrutiny. It's a strange combination of ambition and anonymity; in the words of one commentator, the conservative think tanks are "a conspiracy in plain sight."

If a conspiracy is truly afoot, then the Cato has become the leading cabal of the digital age, the "it" tank. Last year they traded in their brownstone HQ (decorated with oriental rugs and English hunting prints) for a $14 million shimmering "ice cube"-- a glass hive of activity. The Cato philosophy has achieved a remarkably high profile because it is, in a word, marketable. Cato scholars consider themselves classical or

CYBERIA

Founded in 1977, the Cato Institute's

mission is to promote "public policy based on individual liberty, limited government, free markets, and peace." The Cato keeps a sharp eye on digital media. In Regulation, their magazine for Business and Policy, Lawrence Gasman, director of telecommunications and technology studies, says that "future historians of the Clinton administration undoubtedly will regard the passage of the Telecommunications Act of 1996 as one of its greatest achievements." Read on.

"market" liberals when pushed (handily explained in document called "How to Label the Cato"). It's a reworking of civil society that concerns itself mostly with civility and autonomy: property rights, mobility, free speech. Executive VP David Boaz gets to the heart of matter: "None of us is smarter than the 200 million people operating in the marketplace. It's the politics of humility."

Boaz himself is a testament to Cato's overwhelming success. Like the other starlet of the neocon dynasty, Dinesh D'Souza, Boaz has only a B.A. (in American History from Vanderbilt), but as he says, the Cato concerns itself "with qualifications, not credentials." A candid charmer, he has a knack for prefiguring public debate; his work on saving the inner city and school choice preceded the current discussion by four years.

With a combination of free market sensibility and technological savviness, the Cato "Inc. tank" scores big with the major players in the computer industry. Sun Microsystems CEO Scott McNealy and TCI's John Malone are patrons, and even Wired editors have found a friendly forum for their ideas. Louis Rosetto spoke at the Cato's benefactors' meeting in Puerto Rico and contributing writer Charles Platt gave the metaphorically-impaired keynote address at the Internet futures conference. ("'Information Superhighway' is inadequate," Platt argued, "the Internet is more like a motel off that highway with lots of rooms.") It comes as no surprise to find that Lawrence Gasman, the head of the Telecommunications division, runs his own consulting business, since Cato's politics are perfectly tailored for the digital entrepreneur. But, counters Boaz, it is by no means exclusive to them. They even managed to persuade Miss Manners she was a libertarian. "We had her over for lunch and told her," says Boaz, "and I think she sort of understood."

In fact, the current and growing popularity of libertarianism and the boom in conservative think tanks over the last decade is no coincidence. In the early 80s, "the business elite acquired its own intelligentsia "says Michael Lind (author of the book, "Up From Conservatism"), "in the form of libertarians." According to Lind, the right-wing "brain trust scheme" was hatched late 1970s by a clique of powerful conservatives like corporate raider William E. Simon and ex-leftist Irving Kristol. Simon, who had been treasury secretary under Nixon and Ford and then, in 1976, became president of the John M. Olin Foundation (one of the most lavish conservative caches), was determined to funnel the growing resources of the business elite into conservative coffers. Simon believed "the only thing that can save the Republican Party. . .is a counterintelligentsia."

Joined with Kristol, Simon worked to channel funds to scholars, social scientists and journalists who would see the connection between political and economic liberty. And their work would, in Simon's words, "dissent from a dominant socialist-statist collectivist orthodoxy which prevails in much of the media, and in most of our large universities."

Needless to say, it worked. By the 1980, a handful of new conservative think tanks permeated Washington and penetrated into the policy-drafting process. The most powerful, the Heritage Foundation (created in 1973), was the brainchild of congressional staffers and conservative publicists, including direct-mail wizard Paul Weyrich. As the richest think tank with $25 million in annual revenue, Heritage scholars outspend all the competitors promoting their ideas -- some of which are, in a word, objectionable. In his book, Lind saves some particular ire for Heritage; he recalls with horror Weyrich's off-hand suggestion to inject rat poison into illegal drugs.

Most of the think tanks have similar genesis stories -- a conservative "archangel" simply decides to start one. Edward Harrison Crane III, who was the head of the moribund Libertarian Party, secured the backing of the Kansas oil magnate Charles Koch in 1977 to start an "implementation group" which became the Cato. They courted scholars and policy advisors "friendly" to their philosophy. "Do we hire socialists here?" says the Boaz, "No, and one reason is because they don't understand the economy. It would be like hiring a flat-earth geographer." The Koch family, which has deep ties to Dole (detailed in a recent issue of The Nation), continues to lavish funds from its multiple foundations to create what scholars testified 30 times before Congress. "The Republicans hadn't held a hearing in 40 years," explains Boaz, "They had a lot of ground to make up." In addition, they made 7 radio and TV appearances, drafted 8 op-ed pieces (almost all to the Wall Street Journal), and were cited 22 times in news stories. House Majority Leader Dick Armey will occasionally stop by for lunch, and two scholars even left to join his Joint Economic Committee.

Who wouldn't be seduced? For the academics and policy wonks now employed there, the Cato offers a chance to work basically unmolested in the company of other intellectuals who agree with you long before you've even spoken. In a city already spellbound by power, at least the Cato wears its politics on its cufflinked sleeve. And a think tank with a penthouse can't be all bad.

Except that the public rarely knows what conversations take place in the penthouse or what ramifications these discussions will have for their own lives. Unlike lobbyists -- universally vilified for pushing a narrow agenda -- think tanks retain an aura of scholarly impartiality, which is one reason why the dreaded moniker of the beltway ("special interests") just doesn't really stick to the Cato's ice cube. Mike Deaver-style excesses are studiously avoided; Cato scholars are much more likely to appear in the op-ed pages than on the cover of Time in a Jaguar. And the institutional emphasis protects the think-tankers from the scandal sheets: some might accuse Cato of boasting too loudly of its success, but no one will catch the "it" tank whispering its secrets into some call girl's ear.

David Boaz can't call out the US Armed forces, nor does Cato control the money supply. But as any libertarian will tell you, in an information economy, the knowledge workers rule the roost. You'd think the Left intelligentsia -- with all its "knowledge is power" sloganeering -- might want in on the think-tank action too, though perhaps they're content with their remote academic cloisters. With the Cato, the Heritage, AEI, and the rest, the conservative movement has assembled a small army of info warriors within the Beltway, fighting the good fight steadily behind the scenes. The question is whether the liberals have the resources -- or the consensus -- to launch a counter-offensive.

(September 26, 1996)

**FEEDLINE**

FEED Contributing Editor Gary Chapman writes in to say: "There are many progressive thinktanks in the U.S.: the Institute for Policy Studies, the Center for Budget and Policy Priorities, the Center for Defense Information, the Economic Policy Institute... Obviously, of course, these organizations and institutions don't have the financial resources of their conservative counterparts..."

Click here to post your responses in our Feedbag discussion area.

links to resources online where books or other products can be purchased. Cyberia, on the other hand, has links to Web resources. In a short blurb under each label, the editors at *Feed* solve one of the most basic problems of hypertext – the inability to see through the link before following it across the Web. They solved this problem by simply explaining where the reference leads and cutting out the blind link-hopping that most hypertext requires of readers. This description can be a few words or a whole paragraph. By eliminating links from the text entirely, the editors and designers at *Feed* have effectively removed the obstacles of hypertext for their readers, while still exploiting the most dynamic aspects of the medium.

**The New York Times** <www.nytimes.com>: The Web site of the Gray Lady separates out its links, but differently from *Feed*'s method. In this example, the page designers

> "It is our belief that customers should have access to all books in print," she said. "The business we are in is about ideas and giving people access to ideas through books."
>
> ---
>
> **Related Sites**
> Following are links to the external Web sites mentioned in this article. These sites are not part of The New York Times on the Web, and The Times has no control over their content or availability. When you have finished visiting any of these sites, you will be able to return to this page by clicking on your Web browser's "Back" button or icon until this page reappears.
>
> - American Library Association Banned Books site
> - American Civil Liberties Union Banned Books site
> - American Booksellers Association Banned Books site
> - BiblioBytes Banned Books site
> - Amazon.com's Banned Book site
> - Banned Books Exhibit
>
> Home | Sections | Contents | Search | Forums | Help
>
> Copyright 1996 The New York Times Company

have placed links at the end of a story, creating footnotes for further Web surfing. Unfortunately, much of the context that *Feed*'s links offer is lost here, since these links are merely listings of related Web sites, without explanation or specific reference to parts of the story. Still, the *Times* model allows readers to explore beyond the article after they have finished. Readers are hit with choices at the appropriate time, and they don't have to backtrack through the content trying to remember which links they wanted to follow.

However, the *Times* also betrays its insecurity about its readers' Web savviness by telling them at the end of each story, "These sites are not part of The New York Times on the Web, and The Times has no control over their content or availability." Don't apologize for the rest of the Web. And don't assume that content is worthless because it isn't yours. Well-written capsules of information about links will provide your readers with all they need to know about where they're going. Begging them to come back doesn't work either. If your site is compelling, they'll be back after they've checked out your links.

**HotWired** <www.hotwired.com/road/95/48/ index5a.html>: Playing with the *Feed* model of moving links to the margins, at HotWired we moved links from the text of a piece on Ecuador into the margin and gave readers further explanation about where the links would lead. This maintained the continuity of the story, and it also worked well from a design perspective. Readers instantly could sense the piece's depth by scanning the left margin.

We still struggled with how much explanation to give each link. We didn't want to fill the margins with paragraph after paragraph of link descriptions. But we felt the need to

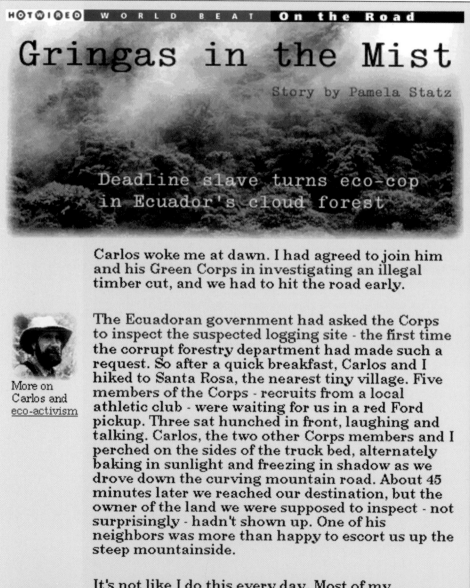

HOT⊙WIRED   W O R L D   B E A T   **On the Road**

# Gringas in the Mist

Story by Pamela Statz

Deadline slave turns eco-cop
in Ecuador's cloud forest

Carlos woke me at dawn. I had agreed to join him and his Green Corps in investigating an illegal timber cut, and we had to hit the road early.

More on
Carlos and
eco-activism

The Ecuadoran government had asked the Corps to inspect the suspected logging site - the first time the corrupt forestry department had made such a request. So after a quick breakfast, Carlos and I hiked to Santa Rosa, the nearest tiny village. Five members of the Corps - recruits from a local athletic club - were waiting for us in a red Ford pickup. Three sat hunched in front, laughing and talking. Carlos, the two other Corps members and I perched on the sides of the truck bed, alternately baking in sunlight and freezing in shadow as we drove down the curving mountain road. About 45 minutes later we reached our destination, but the owner of the land we were supposed to inspect - not surprisingly - hadn't shown up. One of his neighbors was more than happy to escort us up the steep mountainside.

It's not like I do this every day. Most of my mornings begin with a walk down cracked, dirty sidewalks to my job in San Francisco, where I spend long days grappling with a million deadlines. But in mid-October, my friend Allison and I traveled to visit my sister Sandy, her husband,

More on
Andean
agriculture

It's not like I do this every day. Most of my mornings begin with a walk down cracked, dirty sidewalks to my job in San Francisco, where I spend long days grappling with a million deadlines. But in mid-October, my friend Allison and I traveled to visit my sister Sandy, her husband, Carlos, and their two children at their bed and breakfast on 1,000 acres, high in Ecuador's Intag Cloud Forest Reserve.

Three years earlier, their property had been invaded by a neighboring landholder. Though Carlos had owned the tract of forest for more than a dozen years, his neighbor had torched about 20 acres of the endangered ecosystem and planted corn. He didn't plan to harvest it - he was out to lure the spectacled bear, one of several endangered species native to the Intag. The scheme worked all too well: he killed one of the bears and sold its gall bladder to a dealer in the Asian medicine trade.

More on
CORDAVI

When Carlos and Sandy sued, their neighbor allegedly bribed the first judge. They appealed and won, but they're still awaiting a final ruling from Quito. Their lawyers, Byron Real and Marcela Enriquez, are the founders of CORDAVI, Ecuador's first public interest environmental law firm. Through Byron and Marcela, Carlos and Sandy were able to raise money to organize the Green Corps.

More on the
cloud forest

That's how I came to be staggering up this mountainside. I ushered everyone ahead of me. Knowing I'd be the slowest climber, I thought it best that I be last. Our guide, a woman wearing a skirt and tiny black shoes, walked up the steep trail as if on a leisurely stroll. My high-tech hiking boots didn't give me the traction I needed, but one of the Green Corps helped pull me up the mountain. The elevation took its toll, but with every ragged breath, I reminded myself that it wasn't every day I could go to battle for a cloud forest.

More: The bone-rattling ride

at least indicate whether a link led to more of the same story or to a resource on the Web. Of course, we felt no compulsion to add *New York Times*–like disclaimers.

Be creative when linking, and be in control of the power it affords you. Your goal at this level is communication, not navigation. Don't distract your readers with links. Use links to enhance your message, both visually and conceptually, adding depth and dynamism to static pages.

Hypertext is the most powerful innovation available to you in Web publishing. Don't abuse it.

## The value-added link

Since the Web is slow, clicking is a commitment. Users learn to be wary of links. Rampant poor linking punishes users for trusting you. It wastes their time and interrupts their experience and stream of consciousness.

Readers make a split-second decision when they encounter a link: What's going to happen when they click? Will the link lead to more information about the subject at hand? Does it lead to a simple definition or an entire Web site? Links give virtually no information about what's behind them. Giving your readers an idea of what they'll get by clicking on a link is a big favor – one that will be much appreciated.

By paying careful attention to your linking style and intelligently embedding your links into your text or blurbs, you shouldn't have to rely on the obvious tactics employed by first-time Web designers. Don't tell readers to "click here" in a text link. Not only does that lack imagination, but it also shows a general misunderstanding of the medium of electronic publishing. How do you know that readers can click? Their browser might take voice commands or they might use a touch-sensitive screen – or who knows?

Likewise, don't move readers through hypertext by telling them where things are. Links are obvious to all but the most inexperienced of Web surfers, and telling users "More information is available here" or "To see the movie, click here" assumes they know nothing about how their browser works. Leave those tutorials for the instruction manual and help pages. Don't describe the technology, and don't be condescending. Give your readers the context they need to make their decisions.

*Linking Editorially*

When including your links in text, craft the pointer with the same care an author takes when crafting a sentence. One crucial technique to keep in mind is *where* the link is placed in the sentence. By carefully matching the word you highlight with the additional content you're linking to, you can give your readers clues about where they will go if they click.

Some examples:

The crowd scrutinized the candidate's comments.

This link might lead to biographical information on the candidate or the candidate's Web page. Notice that the link doesn't include the possessive – just the noun is the link. Same goes for any punctuation, including periods, commas, and quotation marks.

The crowd scrutinized the candidate's comments.

This link goes to an expanded account of the comments the candidate made.

The crowd scrutinized the candidate's comments.

From this link, the reader should be taken to a picture, movie, or description of the crowd.

*Hypertext: The Next Generation*

The hypertext link was the whole reason for the Web in the first place. Combining a comprehensive addressing system (which we now know as URLs) with a simple method for pointing one resource at another was the foundation on which the Web was built.

Links weren't always this stupid. In fact, the early architects had a much broader vision for how hyperlinking would take place. Links could serve as more than simple anchors, shining in their bright blue colors and waiting for users to click. Links would also be able to add information to a document that wouldn't necessarily be displayed to the reader.

Ideally, hyperlinks should enable everything from providing context for Web search engines to providing a mechanism for two-way links. This is important stuff, and you should know about it. See the official specification on the W3C Web site at <www.w3.org/pub/WWW/TR/WD-htmllink>.

## Beyond the HREF

Editorial context for links is just the beginning. Learning some technical hacks will let you truly give your readers a glimpse of where they're about to go.

Scripting languages such as JavaScript give you some control of a user's browser. Take this opportunity to guide readers. In a status bar at the bottom of the page, browsers let users preview the URL that a link leads to. But expecting users to decode the arcane structure of URLs to guess where they're going is simply unrealistic. For both Netscape and Internet Explorer users, you can embed a little script into your anchor tags that replaces the URL preview in the browser's display area. You can write straightforward descriptions of where links lead, avoiding cryptic URLs.

Write these pointer descriptions as if they were headlines. Don't try to tease your readers into following the links. Instead, offer them useful information that helps them decide whether they should leave their current focus to dig deeper into an area of interest.

*Get Rid of URLs*
**What information does a URL give your readers? Even if they can decode the arcane machine and path names, it really tells them very little. Instead, with JavaScript you can use any text you like to replace the URL in the little status window of your reader's browsers. Adding a few simple scraps of code will offer clarity to obscure links.**

```
<A HREF="http://www.foo.com/bar.html" onMouseOver="window.status='More information
on FooBar'; return true">
```

Authors and designers can push the limitations in today's Web only so far. Eventually, the technology must advance and mature, allowing content providers to develop and explore new interfaces to hypertext.

For example, when you pass your cursor over a link, the pointer turns into a hand signifying the ability to click. But why just one alternative? Why doesn't the cursor turn into a projector when the link goes to a video file or a camera when the link points at a picture? Couldn't the pointer turn to a different shape if the link left the current Web site? Why not add even more information? The cursor could change colors, fading into gray based on the age of a link, or it could shift in size, based on the length of the linked content. Of course, the best solution would be to allow designers to create their own separate cursors for different mouseOver events, thereby offering as much context as possible for the audience.

The example above simply adds the code to a link reference. There's no need to define a huge script in the head of your document or to link to an external suite of scripts. These few commands tell the browser to display the supplied text in the status window. Using *onMouseOver* triggers the code to change the *window.status* to the supplied text, "More information on FooBar," only when the cursor passes over the link. The *return true* forces the browser to remove the default URL display. This little hack will only work on newer JavaScript-enabled browsers. Older browsers, however, will safely ignore the code and simply display the address as they always do.

ABOUT
US

*"a fish, a barrel, and a smoking gun"*
*for 11 October 1996. Updated every WEEKDAY.*

## Lifestyles of the Rich and Famous

The fashion arc may swing from

the hood to the <u>mall</u> and back

again, but if news trends lack a

discernible point of origin,

they do have a definable end.

And any media junkie (count us

as mainliners) knows the point

at which a trend story has been

beaten to death enough to be

considered passé: when it

makes the cover of *Time*

magazine. At Suck, there's a

different standard for the dead

trend horses we choose to flay.

### Breaking the rules

Finally, once you understand the problems of hypertext, you can explore its limits and improve your Web site by doing so. Remember that the Web may have been created in the ivory tower of academia, but it's for all of us now. Pay attention when you surf, and see how people use hypertext not only for navigation and depth but also for fun.

**Suck** <www.suck.com>: This sarcastic site – and sibling of HotWired's – uses hypertext for its own brand of biting humor. Since understanding its content requires some Web and industry savvy, *Suck* can demand a little more understanding of the workings of hypertext than, say, *The New York Times* can. So the writers are talking about the Web as "a wasteland filled with lame, overpriced corporate Web sites," you can be sure the link will take you to what they think are particularly egregious examples of such sites. But often the editors are even subtler. For example, when a column said, "One is forced to suspect that bodies like those of most Calvin Klein models are – without some help – just as unachievable," the linked words *some help* pointed to a discussion of steroids. There is no context for the link, no navigational clues for the reader – it breaks all the rules – and works perfectly.

**When the haze of enchantment with hypertext has faded and you've learned its dangers and what it offers, you can take control of its capabilities to make your site smarter, clearer, deeper, and – if you're really good – funnier.**

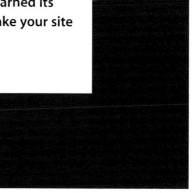

# Beware Multimedia

Computers can amaze us with multimedia. They can swoop through 3-D worlds, pump digital video across the screen, blast stereo sound through the speakers. They can dance and bounce and sing.

The Web, however, cannot.

Technology developers are doing their best to stuff the network full of the jaw-dropping, heart-stopping multimedia that makes computers jump off the shelf and into consumers' homes. But once the machines are out of the box and jacked into the Web, these new users will find streaming video that merely trickles, compatibility problems that keep them up all night installing plug-ins, and hidden security holes behind every click.

Multimedia is compelling. It demos well. But is it the best vehicle for your message? Should you be investing in the time and resources required to package your content in this attractive wrapper? You need a strategy for evaluating the endless flavors of technology out there, and you need to know the basics of delivering these experiences to your audience.

In the end, with a careful balance of appropriate multimedia, your users should be greeted with a seamless experience. But if you don't do your homework, your site will become a technological barrier. Or worse, your audience will lose out on the richness of your content because of your lackluster presentation.

Each of the enticing bells and whistles in computer-based design – full-motion video, CD-quality audio, dazzling animations – exacts its own price. So when is the benefit worth the cost?

### On the grid

Should you use Shockwave? Would a GIF be better? Should you choose streaming audio? Would a block of text do the trick?

Comparing each particular technology's bandwidth requirements to its level of degradability allows you to make informed and intelligent choices about Web-based

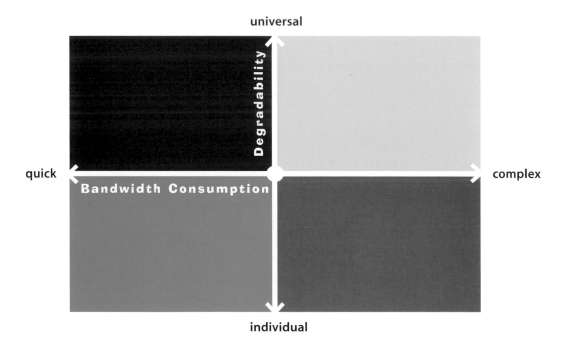

multimedia. It's the same as page design: fast, universal technologies win over the slow and the proprietary.

To help picture the comparison, create a grid with bandwidth consumption on one axis and degradability on the other. Orient yourself in the grid. You already know the benefits of highly degradable content (it stands up across lots of browsers and devices or offers some lesser version of its content to browsers that don't support particular features). On the bandwidth axis, of course, lower is better. Faster formats that travel in compact files will be toward the left, on the low end of the bandwidth line.

We'll use an average audience for an average Web site in this example. But you can position your acceptable range on the grid anywhere, depending on your target audience or special equipment circumstances. An intranet application, for instance, can assume a very narrowly defined amount of bandwidth and installed software among its users. Or maybe you are positioning your site for first-time users of the Net; in that case, speed is of utmost importance, while blowing their minds with motion is a low priority.

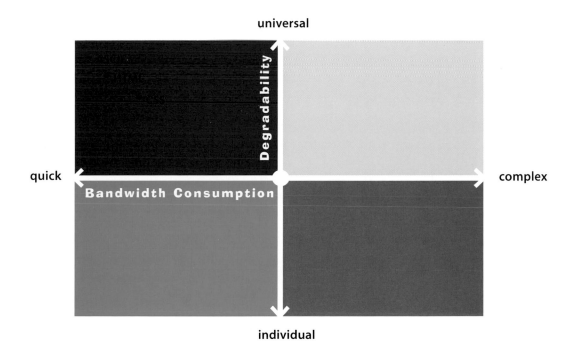

On the grid, moving from the upper left-hand corner (the most accessible content delivered quickly) to the lower right (complex and multimedia-rich experiences that demand a fatter pipe and disappoint ill-equipped users), you can see how benefits and liabilities are often inextricably tied together in Web delivery formats.

The Web's core technologies embody Web values — low bandwidth use and great degradability. ASCII text, the simplest format, falls at the extreme upper left; it transmits nearly instantly and has an almost universal ability to display on any device. The closest neighbor to ASCII's austerity is HTML, which is only slightly less compatible across multiple platforms – consider Web-enabled pagers or cellular phone displays – but is just as fast, since it is still basically text. Moving toward the center of the grid, cascading style sheets (CSS) offer more power to designers, but at a higher cost than HTML. Style sheets are currently much less widely compatible, but they're still as compact and quickly transmitted as the other text-based formats. Style sheet technology still sits above the center line on the degradability range, however, since browsers that don't support style sheets can usually safely ignore them.

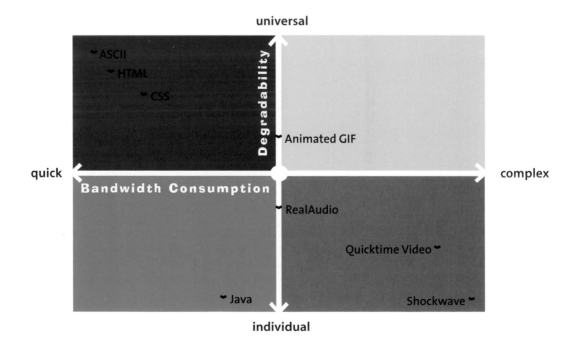

Plotting more-advanced technologies on the chart shows the obvious drawbacks of beefier features. A face-off between interactive technologies like Macromedia's Shockwave and Sun's Java programming language shows them to be equally lacking in degradability, yet differing widely in bandwidth consumption. GIF animations are markedly more degradable and substantially lighter on bandwidth than either Java or Shockwave. If all you wanted to do was to create a simple, stationary animation, you could, in theory, use any of these three technologies. Looking at the grid, though, tells you that a GIF animation, at this point, is your best bet.

A trend emerges: Technologies that require hefty bandwidth tend also to require advanced browsers or special software and to degrade rather ungracefully. But often the level of interactivity and richness increases along the same lines, making these formats enticing despite their limitations. It's a trade-off.

The many popular audio and video formats are a vivid example of this trade-off at work. Progressive Networks' RealAudio, a streaming audio format, can run under very little bandwidth – as little as 1 Kbps – while still maintaining some level of usability. Yet, at that rate, experiencing the scratchy, popping audio is equivalent to listening to the radio over the telephone. Bandwidth use is optimized at quality's expense. Apple's QuickTime video, on the other hand, gives both a smooth audio track and the slickness of full-motion video. But by choosing QuickTime, you're asking your visitors to patiently wait for a movie to slowly download so they'll have an intense, lifelike payoff. Quality wins out over bandwidth.

## Putting it into play

We've used multimedia with varying degrees of success on HotWired. Our coverage of digital art in our early Renaissance channel, for example, demanded that we push the multimedia envelope. In a feature on the favorite photographs of contemporary artists <www.hotwired.com/renfeatures/96/13/index5a.html>, we combined frames, images, text, and streaming audio to offer our audience a complete experience.

Originally, the images were mixed into a frame-based layout to provide clear navigation through the story. After

*While You Wait…*
**You know how your dentist puts out all those magazines for you to read while you're waiting to get your teeth worked on? Do the same if you're using QuickTime on your page. If you embed a video, make sure you pay attention to your first frame – people are going to be looking at it for a while (quite a while, if the average Web-based digital video experience is any indication). Give them something interesting to stare at. Anything is better than the alternative: watching that download indicator creep along.**

## The People

John Baldessari,
*artist*

David Byrne,
*musician*

David Corey,
*college professor*

Aida Rivera,
*AIDS activist*

Joan Rivers,
*comedienne*

Bruce Weber,
*photographer*

# Moving Stills

## Is there a photograph that obsesses you?

Marvin Heiferman and Carole Kismaric asked 69 people – some famous, some unknown – to select the one image that most "seduced, inspired, taught, frightened, amused, offended, obsessed, informed, or provoked them." The result is *Talking Pictures*, a book and traveling exhibition showing at the Los Angeles County Museum of Art through June. Its collection of images, essays, and audio clips proves that in a world saturated with images, a single photo can still leave an indelible mark.

"We made it clear that the picture could come from anywhere – from a family album, a movie, an advertisement, television, a newspaper, even from a matchbook," Heiferman and Kismaric write. It is the wide array of personalities and images and the intimate ties between them that make this project surprising. Post-it Note inventor Arthur L. Fry, for instance, selects a 500x magnification of his ubiquitous adhesive strip, while corporate administrative assistant Gina Greco chooses a live-concert photo of Axl Rose. In the book, only a few pages separate G. Gordon Liddy's choice, a photo of three dead US Marines, from Dennis Hopper's, an Henri Cartier-Bresson photograph titled *Sunday on the Banks of the Mane*. Each person writes and talks about the power of the chosen photos.

To give you the feel of *Talking Pictures*, we have posted six audio and visual excerpts, and are providing a space for you to add your own photo.

By Sarah Borruso

*Talking Book*
A Lookout Book, in association with
The International Center of Photography, New York
Chronicle Books
275 Fifth Street
San Francisco, CA 94103
(800) 722 6657

## Discuss *Talking Pictures*

interviewing the various artists, the editors decided that the feature would be much more effective if our readers could hear the descriptions, as well as read them. Thus, the commentary was digitized and offered in the RealAudio streaming format, which would automatically scale to a user's connected speed. More important, the audio was optional, embellishing the piece rather than being a requirement. The combination of low-resolution graphics, discrete chunks of content in frames, and optional audio made the feature work on several levels for nearly all readers.

We've experimented on the other end of the multimedia spectrum as well. When Apple first released its QuickTime plug-in, we took the opportunity to experiment with digital video as delivered via the Web. Instead of offering a "video-on-demand" experience, we tried to create a sort of multi-

Surfing as jeff.

RENAISSANCE ON TOUR

John Baldessari (b. 1931) is an artist whose works have been exhibited in museums and galleries worldwide. His teaching career at California Institute of the Arts has influenced generations of experimental artists.

Choose another photograph.

An untitled movie production still, 1960s. C. Kenneth Lobben

## Commentary from John Baldessari:
[RealAudio 14.4 | 28.8]

media collage. Spun with a political theme for our Netizen channel, the piece mixed clips of 1996 presidential candidates, other politicians, and journalists with propagandalike slogans over a driving techno beat. Users could control each square of video if they desired, and a standard QuickTime button allowed them to mute the soundtrack.

**The Net**

Pundits. Pols.
Talking heads.

They can run,
but they can't hide.

The Netizen:
An unorthodox
antidote to politics
as usual.

**So many**

**reporters,**

N E T I Z E N
www.netizen.com

Nothing happening? Double–click on a box to get something going. Click once to make it stop.

This feature was far from degradable or bandwidth-friendly. Checking in at nearly 2 megabytes, the page would take a modem user more than fifteen minutes to load – not exactly instant gratification. But we put this offering in the context of a demo, warning users of the download requirements and assuming a powerful, feature-laden browser. The result was an intranetlike example of a compelling multimedia experience for our high-end users.

If you have Apple's QuickTime plug-in installed and a fast connection to the Net (or a lot of patience), check out the Netizen demo of this piece at <www.webmonkey.com/webmonkey/demo/96/32/anna.demo.html>. If you'd like to find out how we went about building it, visit <www.webmonkey.com/webmonkey/demo/96/32/index4a.html>. For a screenshot only, go to <www.webmonkey.com/webmonkey/demo/96/32/anna.screenshot.html>.

But you're only getting started. You've compared a format's bandwidth appetite and its degradability against its features. Now you need to factor in how the technology is *distributed*. After all, the most fantastic format, no matter how small and degradable, is pointless if no one can use it.

## Netscape falters: the broken icon

When Netscape released its much anticipated second version of Navigator in 1995, a huge wave of hype accompanied its newly developed "plug-in architecture." Using a system long familiar to Adobe Photoshop and Quark XPress users, the company aimed at opening up a whole new market of multimedia content on the Web by building Navigator to be compatible with a broad range of small, feature-enhancing extensions that would take the place of helper apps. The idea was to have a simple way of integrating players for any sort of electronic media – video, sound, animation, or any other file format, including word processing files, CAD renderings, and even speech – into the Web browser. Developers bought in, and soon hundreds of plug-ins flooded the marketplace, nearly all for free. Netscape's Navigator was now theoretically the only application you would need to view any content on the Web.

But despite that glut of plug-ins, nobody actually produced any *content* with them. With the unfortunate exception of massive Shockwave files shoveled over from the world of CD-ROM publishing and the occasional in-line QuickTime movie, virtually no content providers embraced the embedding of plug-in media.

Why? Blame the awful interface Netscape developed to handle the vast array of possible plug-ins. If you were to embed, say, some sort of streaming video clip on your homepage, your visitors would be required to have the right plug-in for that particular type of video (and there are dozens of types of video alone). Since most Web surfers probably lacked your particular brand of video plug-in, they would be confronted by a blank area where the clip was supposed to display, with a small, broken plug-in icon loaded in its center. Then would come the inevitable error dialog box (saying something to the effect of "Unknown media type. Ignore? Info?"). Users choosing to ignore the media could surf on with the broken icon.

But if they chose Info, they would be whisked away to ... yes ... Netscape's Web site and a long list of the available plug-ins, with no clue as to which one to download. If they happened to pick the right one, they would have to download it, uncompress the file, move it into the appropriate directory in their Netscape directory, and then quit and

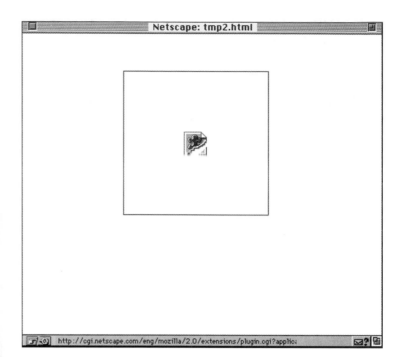

*Sniffing for Plug-ins*

Attempts to provide users with a seamless multimedia experience have been only marginally successful. Using Netscape's JavaScript, some content providers have written functions that peek inside the Plugins folder to see if the user has, say, Shockwave installed. If so, down comes the movie. If not, you can replace the presentation with an image. It's a kluge, but it will work in a pinch. Of course, the problem remains: if nobody has the plug-in, nobody sees your multimedia. But at least you can avoid the hideous broken image.

Here's the code to add to your page:

```
<SCRIPT LANGUAGE="javascript">
var plugged = testForPlugin('application/x-director');

function testForPlugin(Plugin) {
   Plugin = Plugin.toLowerCase();
   var Found = false, i, j;
   for (i = 0; i < navigator.plugins.length; i++) {
      for (j = 0; j < Math.round(navigator.plugins[i].length); j++) {
         if (navigator.plugins[i][j].type == Plugin) {
               Found = true;
          }
      if (Found);
        }
     }
   return (Found);
}
if (plugged) {
   document.writeln('Put the embed tag for your plug-in here');
} else {
   document.writeln('Put the alternate HTML here');
}
</SCRIPT>
```

restart the browser and surf back to your page. The scheme failed miserably, much to the disappointment of plug-in developers and the scant few content providers who bothered with the technology.

The last thing you want on your pages is broken icons. And you don't want to drive users away with massive downloads and installation nonsense. Do a little research and make sure your multimedia efforts are worthwhile.

### Microsoft counters with ActiveX

Microsoft soon followed with its own solutions to the multimedia delivery problem. Hoping to capitalize on a huge investment in object linking and embedding (OLE) technology, the company introduced an alternative to the plug-in interface: ActiveX.

OLE allows programs written for Windows to be embedded into other programs. For example, before OLE, you could add a spreadsheet created in Excel to a report written in Microsoft Word. But using OLE, updating the embedded

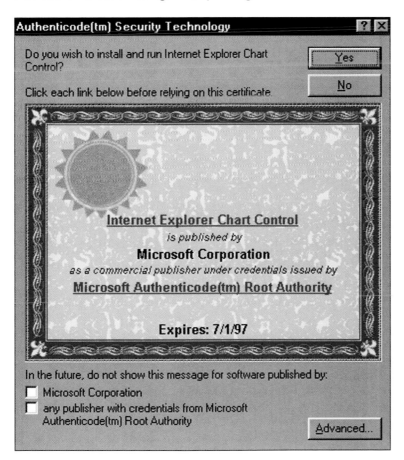

spreadsheet from within Word is as easy as clicking on it. Your Word toolbars and menus turn into Excel toolbars and menus (since both programs are OLE-enabled) and you can theoretically continue working without interruption.

ActiveX was simply a way of making Microsoft's Web browser, Internet Explorer, an OLE container like Word or Excel, so any sort of content could then be embedded in a Web page.

The key for content providers was the automatic installation of ActiveX controls on users' machines. Users would simply surf to a page, be presented with a dialog box informing them of the installation process, and immediately view the intended content. Since controls were permanently installed, like Netscape plug-ins (and not just temporarily cached, like HTML pages or images), users could build up a collection of popular media players simply by surfing from site to site. Eventually, popular multimedia formats like RealAudio, QuickTime video, and VRML would be a seamless experience for everyone using Internet Explorer.

But this utopian dream was short-lived. Two significant drawbacks to the technology kept if off most pages across the Web. First, in truly practical terms, content providers wishing to create ActiveX controls for their viewing audience had to make some pretty significant platform decisions. ActiveX gives developers access to powerful operating system components. This means they can control native OS multimedia routines or simple windowing and dialog box functions built into the user's platform. This power comes at the cost of compatibility, requiring an ActiveX control to be rewritten for all platforms the developer or content provider is inclined to support. That means content must be developed over and over again: for Windows 95, Windows 3.1, Windows NT, Macintoshes, and any other platform that supports ActiveX.

**Muzak for Your Pages**

Ever wanted to add a soundtrack to your Web presentation? Imagine a droning techno beat behind your killer homepage or a soothing ambient collage of sound to accompany your image portfolio. Microsoft, at least, thought it would be a good idea and hacked in a BGSOUND attribute for the <BODY> tag. So now anyone could add whatever introductory or looping sound desired for a page, by using something as simple as this code:

```
<BODY BGSOUND="foo.wav">
```

Beyond the fact that it was completely against standard HTML, Netscape never adopted the syntax. So in the end, you can add this neat little gimmick to your page, but remember that only Internet Explorer users will actually hear the audio. Everyone else will read your content in peaceful silence.

### Enter the publishers

Cross-platform decisions are nothing new to software developers, who have faced the prospect of either choosing one platform and limiting their audience or else finding the resources to write different versions for different operating systems. But these decisions are something totally alien to the world of publishing. Content providers who have come to the Web from traditional forms of publishing are used to the ubiquity of paper, television broadcasts, or AM/FM radio. Everyone can get your content. Period. Not to mention the cross-platform, cross-device, cross-browser freedom that Web developers had come to expect.

As a result, content providers began to align themselves with browser developers. Little banners and logos began to pop up across the homepages of the Web, proclaiming sites to be compatible by saying "Netscape Now!" or "Activate the Internet with Microsoft!" And publishers didn't use these icons as simple suggestions for visitors. These little banners and the technology they represented were the result of carefully negotiated marketing deals between the software companies and the content providers. The Web's unique beauty of being not about proprietary formats but about communication soon fell into grave danger.

And that's where the situation gets a bit troubling. Publishers want new technologies as well as people to view them. Software developers can provide both. But when a company like Microsoft decides not to provide a technology like ActiveX to a customer base like the huge Win3.1 community, a rift grows in the availability of content. Suddenly, some ideas are served only to people with powerful browsers. This is a whole new issue for publishers, and it's a dilemma that everyone is going to have to deal with in a hurry.

## Convenient but insecure

Microsoft promised a largely seamless experience to the user by making ActiveX controls self-installing, and it promised power to the developer by offering access to the inner workings of the operating system. The result, to say the least, is a security nightmare. As users surf the Web, they can encounter any sort of malicious code designed to do damage to their system or to snoop information from their drive or any attached networks. In response, Microsoft introduced the concept of code signing, which uses digital signatures to verify the identity of the content provider and the authenticity of the code. Each time a user hits a page with an ActiveX control, a dialog box informs the user of who is sending what. But after a few pages and accompanying dialog boxes, the safety feature becomes annoying, and a simple selection in the browser Options panel removes it. Now any Web site can install any code in the systems of its visitors without their knowledge.

Even if users did keep the code-checking features in place, it would be trivial to add a sort of time-release routine to the malicious code, causing a system meltdown days or weeks after the page had been visited. And even if a user was able to recover his system, dig into the installed controls, and determine who dropped the bomb, Microsoft suggested appropriate legal action as his recourse. So the user must now bring the malicious author to trial – regardless of geographical location – in an attempt to gain some sort of reimbursement for the damage done. Are you ready to deal with international data-corruption laws to bring suit against a college student with a sick sense of humor?

---

*Don't Use Java for Multimedia*

If ever an Internet technology has been overhyped, it has been Sun's Java. The idea is beautiful, of course – a cross-platform, cross-browser, robust programming language. The power of C++ with the portability of HTML. Write one program and distribute it over the Net to anyone on any computer anywhere. And though the hype may, in fact, play out someday in the software development world, Java shouldn't be used for multimedia.

The first proof-of-concept applets to emerge in Java's early days were simple moving images and animations. Of course, this was before animated GIFs, media plug-ins, and other tricks of the trade. And though animation applets flourished at first, reality relegated multimedia written in Java to a temporary solution at best.

And Java isn't for beginners, either. It's a full-featured programming language – not a quick copy-and-paste hack to your pages. If you're going to get into distributed code, you're going to have to know what you're doing, and you can start at Sun's Java site <www.javasoft.com>.

Again, use the appropriate tools for the job. Java is great for sending applications to users' desktops (our Talk.com chat system, for example, is written in Java). But for creating compelling multimedia content, look elsewhere.

Multimedia on the Web is difficult. You'll have such a wide range of users that it's impossible to know who can see what. And even if they can use your fancy media, will they even bother with the download? In the computer software industry, developers have historically relied on strong platforms and operating systems to deal with problems such as these. But even there, we're without a solution. Both Netscape and Microsoft have let us down, offering multimedia interfaces with such fundamental flaws as to be nearly unusable.

Your choices? In previous chapters, you've seen how to use layered code to create gracefully degrading Web pages. Now we've also built a methodology for evaluating appropriate technologies for those pages. Combine the two strategies, test in as many browsers and platforms as possible, and pray for a future in which streaming video, CD-quality audio, or any other form of media is seamlessly compatible for everyone.

# No Shovelware!:
# New Media Deserves
# New Content

In the early days of television, American radio broadcasters used the new medium in the only way they knew how: they dressed their news announcers in nice suits and stood them in front of a camera to read the day's headlines. It wasn't until years later, when journalists brought cameras with them to cover events as they happened, that television news found its voice and purpose.

We've seen the same sort of shortsighted, inelegant attempts on the Web. Many early Web publishers have failed to embrace new thinking for this new medium.

Trying to reproduce a newspaper layout on a screen, as seen in the *Wall Street Journal Interactive Edition* <wsj.com>, for example, may successfully leverage the paper's familiar, trusted look, but ultimately it fails to exploit the distinguishing qualities of the Web. Why cement your content into printlike columns when screen-based pages can scroll? Why use page numbers – yes, *page numbers* – for a navigation system, as have the dyed-in-the-wool print editors at *Slate* <www.slate.com>, Microsoft's "experimental" online magazine.

Obviously, centuries of different forms of communication needn't be ignored. Rich lessons rest within diverse disciplines like typography, sequential art, and oral storytelling. But while other media can guide us, simply moving methods from one medium to another seldom works.

The truly exhilarating Web sites are the ones that make you think, "Wow, this couldn't be done anywhere else but the Web." *Word* <www.word.com>, with its meticulously designed and consciously paced click-through features, is a great model.

The Web, for all its advantages, challenges designers, authors, and engineers with cripplingly slow speeds, and an archaic lack of typographic and layout control, and a cultural history rooted not in communication but in the obscure discipline of computer science. For a Web site to be successful, its creators must exploit these weaknesses, blending content with creative problem solving to find the very best way to communicate using today's technology. Simply repurposing content from other media – shoveling vast quantities of information from one medium to another without creativity and thought – will fail.

# Follow Your Audience

When I go to my corner video rental store, the guy behind the counter greets me by name and, if he's not too busy, recommends a movie. I rent about a movie a week, and over the course of a year of rentals and conversations, it's gotten so I can rely on him to recommend tapes that will get a thumbs-up from me. Occasionally, he'll take a chance and offer me something in a genre I seldom select, with an actor I rarely care for. And he always guesses right.

Then I stop by the supermarket and do my weekly shopping. A clerk slides my purchases over a scanner, and I slide my bank card through a reader. All of my purchases, along with my identity, are fed into a database where they are compared with my past purchases at that market. Along with my receipt, the clerk passes me a fistful of individually selected coupons that anticipate products I might want, based on what I tend to buy.

Although one is a mom-and-pop business and the other is part of a nationwide chain, both stores have found ways to customize their services to suit me – and both, in very different ways, show that they recognize me as an individual, that not all customers are alike. The Web lets you do this for *your* visitors. What the medium lacks in bandwidth and resolution, it makes up for in precision. Unlike print and TV, when you're working on the Web, you don't have to give everyone the same thing. You have the advantage of seeing who's out there and determining how they use your site and what they want.

To fail to keep tabs on your users and connect with them as individuals is to pass up one of the Web's greatest assets for publishing and business. But to avoid overwhelming visitors with choices, locking them into their perceived tastes, or isolating them, you must intelligently choose when and how to open the lines of communication between your site and your visitors.

### Optional options

There will always be a group of savvy, experienced Web surfers who want to customize their experience on the Web. HotWired's first users, who were largely techie, early-adapter types, easily digested our crude interfaces for content customization and threaded discussions. As greater numbers of less experienced users came online, however, we found that a smaller chunk of our audience was willing to set intricate personal preferences for a single Web site. We, and the whole Web industry, were suddenly dealing with a throng of newbies. HTML authoring tools bragged about software easy enough to use that your grandmother could create a homepage. And Netscape's homepage became the site with the most hits in the world, simply because so few users were savvy enough to customize their browser so that it wouldn't automatically go there when they launched Netscape.

But those tech-friendly Net enthusiasts who came to our early site still make up the Web's most loyal audience, and they are still not satisfied with passive information and entertainment consumption.

So how can you please both the multitude of newbies and the loyal techno-elite? Tread carefully when making assumptions about the level of participation and motivation you can expect from visitors, especially if your success depends on it. Make setting preferences a preference in itself – optional. Pitch the level of participation your site expects from visitors to their level of tech sophistication – and make customization, like your whole site, degradable.

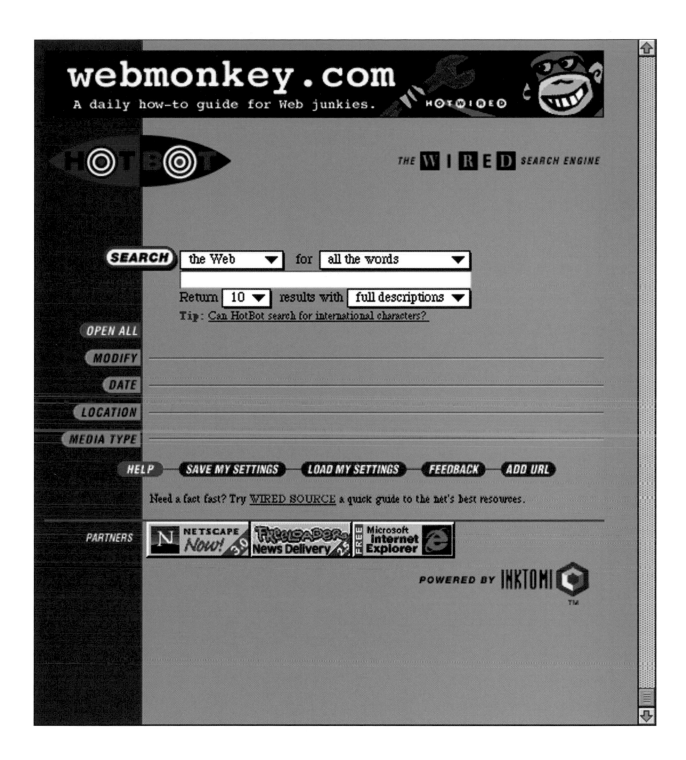

## Scaleable power: HotBot

Our HotBot search engine <www.hotbot.com> makes its customization degradable by hiding powerful personalization features under tabs on its frontdoor. By concealing this complexity behind expandable sections, we are able to keep the initial experience as simple and intuitive as possible for first-time users. Meanwhile, the site's true power — searching by date, media type, location, and so on – is a click away for users who are ready for it.

And we offer power users a way to customize for the long run, enticing them to come back to HotBot rather than turn to our competitors. Once a user has adjusted the interface for her specific needs, she can choose the Save My Settings feature, which places the stored settings in a cookie file on her hard drive (see "Tools as Buttons"). Then, every time she comes back, she automatically sees her own version of HotBot.

*Tools as Buttons*

To preserve the HotBot interface for individual users, the Save My Settings feature needed to trigger a script on the server side. This meant sending the contents of a form (which was, in essence, the current state of HotBot's interface) to the server when the user clicked the button. The problem? Our button was part of a toolbar that was based on an image map – and you can't activate a script with an image map.

HELP — SAVE MY SETTINGS — LOAD MY SETTINGS — FEEDBACK — ADD URL

The solution: using GIFs as buttons has a built-in benefit of sending the coordinates along with the form contents to the server. Therefore, we could trigger the appropriate CGI script based on *where* on the bar a user clicked. The Save My Settings button triggered the save script, whereas the Help button simply caused a CGI to redirect the browser to the appropriate page.

When you learn the capabilities and limitations of your battery of Web formats and tools, you can come up with creative uses to suit unusual combinations of needs.

Really degradable customization gives your site an intriguing depth. The HotBot site works perfectly for first-time visitors, but the longer they stick around, the more they discover they can do and control. And the more choices they set, the more connected and loyal they feel to our site.

## Watch, but don't be Big Brother

Besides letting users tell your site what they want, Web technology lets you watch over your visitors' shoulders and learn their habits and preferences.

It's important to carefully strategize how you'll reveal your observation and its result to visitors, because tracking online identity makes people nervous. George Orwell captured people's fears of invasive technology in *1984*, subtly transforming the then-nascent television – making it work in both directions – to conjure a world in which the government, embodied in Big Brother, kept an eye on every citizen for missteps and subversion.

The Web, like Big Brother's surveillance tool, is built for two-way communication. When you surf to a Web site, your browser asks the server for a page and the server needs to know where to send it. The more a server knows about a client, the better it can tailor what it serves.

*Follow Your Audience*

But two-way communication can go too far. A bug in an early implementation of Netscape's JavaScript allowed unscrupulous page authors to grab the email address of each visitor. If you knew that every Web site grabbed your email address, would you click cavalierly from link to link? Think of the endless spam filling your email in-box.

As it stands, the individual IP address of your machine *is* recorded in the logs of every server you hit. Aggregated, it would give a pretty telling story of your viewing habits that a company could use to market to your specific profile or, perhaps, that someone could use to blackmail you. The trick is to find a balance between custom content and personal privacy.

*Using Server Logs for Fun and Profit*
Lots of interesting information resides in HTTP server logs — if you know what you're looking for.

**Address:** When a user hits your page, the machine he's surfing from is recorded. You can use this information immediately. You could serve different pages (or, in our case, ads) to .com addresses versus .edu addresses. Or send pages in French to .fr addresses. You might urge folks with an aol.com address to find a better server. The possibilities are endless.

### Are you a member?
When we launched HotWired in 1994, our previously untested strategy of asking for a username and a password gave us all the advantages of knowing our visitors. It also unearthed extreme reactions from a Web community sensitive to being watched.

The day we flipped the switch and went live on the Net, all users were greeted with a screen asking them if they were a member or not. Answering no brought you to an HTML form-based registration page. Answering Yes popped up a dialog box that simply asked for a name and a password.

This was new to the Web, and to put it delicately, we received more than a few flames. Some critics accused us of being a clueless proprietary service like America Online, while others questioned the motives behind our ability to track users from page to page.

We settled on authentication in 1994 when we saw how apprehensive early sponsors were about putting money into this young and uncharted medium. We never would have been able to sell advertising on the Web with vague explanations of how hits and page views translate into counting

**Date, time, file size:** As your logs accumulate, date, time, and file size stats are great for judging server load and traffic patterns. Cross-referencing that information with addresses, you could see how European-based traffic affects your San Francisco based Web server. Using date and time, you could also write scripts to greet users with a message like "Good Morning," or "Six more days until we go beta!"

**Referrer:** This entry lists addresses of pages with links that surfers followed to get to your pages. In essence, you've got a long list of the location of every effective link to your pages. You can use this to serve custom content to people who follow specific hypertext pointers. For example, if someone clicks an entry in Yahoo's database to get to your homepage, you can greet them with a specific message just for Yahoo users.

individual users. With an authenticated Web site, we could track unique views of each ad-supported page.

As time progressed and more Web sites began competing for online advertising, HotWired again had an advantage. Since our registration process asked new users for

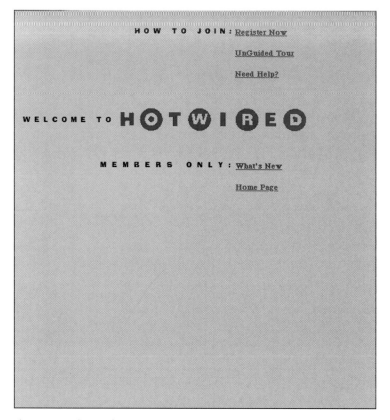

demographic information, we could accurately correlate that information with the pages they later viewed, giving potential advertisers exactly what they wanted – accurate descriptions of readers seeing their advertisement.

We've continued to push the narrowcasting capabilities allowed by user tracking ever since. Our advertisers have the ability to focus on individual countries, Fortune 500 companies, or students. And even beyond focused ad serving, we've been developing algorithms to make the banner model of advertising more intelligent. As a piece of advertising lives on our pages, a database tracks the sort of users who react positively to the banner (by clicking on it) and changes the ad's rotation schedule to reach more members of its most-receptive audience.

What was good for the advertisers was also good for the users. Unlike TV, where children watch car advertisements and men see makeup ads, we could give visitors a better chance of seeing ads for products they actually used or were interested in knowing about.

### The Technology of Tracking

In the Web's short life so far, four technological solutions have been used to track user identity, with varying levels of success.

**Unique session IDs in URLs:** Some of the earliest attempts to track Web users appended a unique code for each user onto the URLs they hit on the site. Time Warner's Path-finder, for example, used addresses like this: <www.path-finder.com/@@sn9xLQYApUVgNXOB/welcome/>. That bizarre string of characters is a sort of serial number that begins to follow the user through the site, allowing Pathfinder to count the number of individual visitors to its Web site and to glean interface effectiveness by studying user page views through the site.

**HTTP authentication:** Another approach, used by HotWired early on, is basic HTTP authentication – a simple form of identification built into Web servers. Each time a browser asks for a file, the server asks for a user name and a password first. If the browser doesn't have them to supply, it asks the user by throwing up a dialog box. All hits from that user to the same server after that will authenticate seamlessly. This technology has many problems, beyond the simple fact that it doesn't scale for users of more than a few Web sites under authentication (you'll spend half your time reminding angry users of their password). Other sites wishing to link to authenticated space immediately produce the identification dialog box in the user's browser completely out of context. Authenticated pages also keep out search engines: these software robots crawl from page to page on the Web, following links and indexing the resulting pages for their catalogs and databases – until they reach authenticated pages, where they choke.

**Magic Cookies:** Netscape developed Magic Cookies, a technology that allows content providers to place a small entry in the preferences file on a visitor's hard drive that can later be retrieved. This may sound trivial, but it's an important way for Web sites to "remember" a visitor on a subsequent visit. Though this process is far easier for users than HTTP authentication, it's also not perfect. Users who switch computers still need to log in at both machines. And there are other problems as well. A media backlash against cookies during the spring of 1996 spurred consumer fears and forced Netscape to add an option for users to deny cookies. Suddenly, content providers couldn't completely rely on the technology.

**Digital certificates:** Though HTTP authentication and Magic Cookies have begun to solve some of the most basic problems with online identity, there is still a margin of error in each technology. As the online community starts to embrace electronic commerce, it's pretty obvious that identity and security are bound together as tightly online as they are in the real world. Personal digital certificates begin to put control of identity in the hands of users. Using public key encryption, digital certificates are issued by a trusted third party to individuals and Web sites. Web surfers can use their IDs for anything from gaining entry to authenticated content to online shopping or banking. The process is relatively simple and takes place in the browser, so users can show the same ID at different Web sites, avoiding the multiple name and password problem.

But we didn't create our complex authentication system for purely commercial concerns. From a design and editorial perspective, knowing who was viewing what page allowed us to build custom features into the site.

Our first experiment with dynamically created content launched shortly after our second homepage. Since we had made use of a text-based navigational map at the bottom of the page, we realized we could change it at will – something that would have been impossible with the image map on the frontdoor we had just abandoned. Authentication and tracking told us which sections of the site each user had visited, and we used that information to generate the navigation map dynamically. When we posted new content, it appeared in boldface text. When a user had visited the page, the label was changed to normal text. The effect worked – our readers could instantly get an overview of what was new for them across our site. This encouraged people to see more of our features and helped orient them in our vast site.

## Keeping it spontaneous

Our next step was to create a customizable version of HotWired's navigation. We moved the What's New feature onto its own separate page, making one central list of fresh content customized for each user. To further focus the list, we created a form-based page where users checked boxes to choose which sections they wanted listed on their own What's New page. Our readers now had the power to create a custom daily HotWired – tailored to their preferences and updated automatically.

A potential problem with relying too heavily on user preferences is that you can stifle the spontaneity of allowing users to stumble across interesting content that they might not have guessed they'd like. We attempted to avoid this

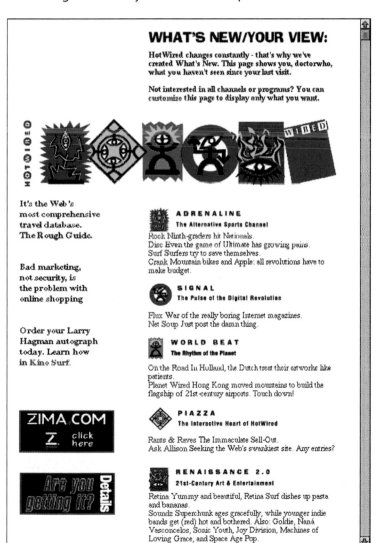

problem on our What's New page by displaying three teaser blurbs across the top of the page that were independent of user preferences. The random-seeming appearance of these blurbs was actually controlled by the weighting system we had built into the script that generated the page. When editors entered the blurbs into our database, they'd assign each one a priority level that determined how often it appeared. Live events received higher rotation than regular weekly content, for example. The combination of user customization with editorially weighted teasers gave our readers an efficient way to navigate through what was becoming an unmanageable amount of daily content.

## Identity for interactivity

Creating an online community forces you to bring out personal identity online. Our Threads system requires participants to log in with a name and a password, as does the chat system we've built at Talk.com. The systems were designed with a faithfulness to that tenet of The Well, "you own your own words." Each individual must be identified with each post or chat. This policy doesn't require you to post under your real name, but even if you do choose a handle to surf with, you'll have to use it consistently and become known over time as that ID. In fact, the only time our active online conversations have really broken down was when some participants used a loophole in the system to post maliciously under an anonymous identity.

Make sure that every time you make a user identify herself, there's a big payoff – either in the form of more-focused content, as in our What's New page, or in a more valuable experience overall, as in our Threads log-in policy. It's a bargain you strike with your visitors. Make sure they know they're getting a good deal.

*Roll Your Own Authentication*
**If the idea of authentication and customization on the Web appeals to you, start experimenting. You don't need root access to your server or even the ability to write a CGI program. In fact, a basic understanding of client-side scripting languages like JavaScript will allow you to begin offering basic custom features to your users. The place to learn, of course, is the Web, and a number of sites that not only teach you JavaScript but also offer freely usable scripts to copy and paste into your pages. To start, check out <www.cookiecentral.com/cookie2.htm>.**

**Then go nuts.**

## Choices, choices

Some sites base their whole identity on user tracking and preference setting. Firefly <www.firefly.com>, developed by MIT Media Lab alumni, asks users to rate lists of music albums and movies, stores their preferences, and compares the information with that of other users. As the database of preferences grows, Firefly is able to match patterns of likes and dislikes among members. After rating a number of entries, the system uses algorithms to generate a list of other movies or albums a user should be interested in, if his tastes continue to resemble those of the other users he has agreed with so far. Blending preference setting into community interactivity, Firefly allows users to search for other Firefly

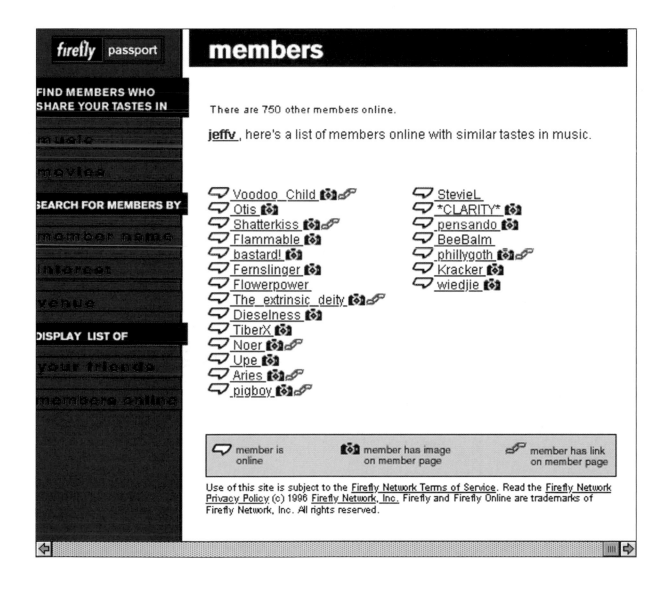

members who have similar tastes and to meet with them in chat rooms.

However, when you visit Firefly, most of your time is spent rating music or movies, selecting "I like that" or "Great stuff" or "Not my thing" for hundreds of choices. This system works well for filtering entertainment offerings, but can you transfer this technology directly over to the daily content consumption of your readers?

A site like HotWired, with its diverse offerings, could in theory benefit from a using a filtering algorithm. With so many choices available to our visitors, any way of adding context in our ocean of content must be a good idea, right? Not entirely.

People who are visiting Firefly are doing so *because* of the interactive nature of the Web pages. They are choosing an experience that will necessitate a response from them. As we've seen, there is one type of user who likes this kind of site; it is not the domain of the uninitiated surfer. Firefly demands considerable interaction before any results can be generated – the antithesis of degradable customization.

Would a visitor to CNN's homepage be interested in filling out page after page of preferences just to see today's headlines? Our experience tells us that most visitors are simply interested in our content right up front. Maybe one in a hundred users will eventually develop enough interest to build some sort of personal profile, and those users are our most loyal readers. The point is never to make this sort of customizability mandatory.

## Personalization = isolation?

Critics of personalized media have wondered what is lost when everyone no longer gets the same mix of news and information in the same order. If a newspaper is created solely on my interests, they argue, then I don't get the value of a common stream of information with my neighbors and my community.

The job of editors of all types is to filter information for you, to let their knowledge of events and context guide you toward what is important. A major difference between reading the *Washington Post* and reading Associated Press stories straight off the wire is that the *Post*'s editors have done you the service of organizing and prioritizing the sea of news. Asking readers to do that work themselves can actually subtract value from your site rather than add it.

What's called for is a finely tuned mix of professionally presented content and customizability. The half-hour television newscast tries to appeal to the lowest common denominator in order to entice the largest number of viewers to sit through the broadcast – too broad. But a personal news service might never tell you that Martians have invaded Earth, since you didn't select the Science and Technology preference – absurdly narrow.

My video store guy knows the power of custom content, information filtering, and personalized information delivery. Of course, he just considers it good customer service. Same goes for the big supermarket – its goal is to make buying easier for me, even if my identity is merely a number encoded on a magnetic strip.

Your job as a content provider is the same. You need to incorporate layered, degradable customization into your sites and to keep a close – but uninvasive – eye on your visitors. By doing so, you'll be combining all the principles of smart Web authoring. You'll be creating simple interfaces that let your readers surf quickly through your content. You'll be able to flatten your site, subverting hierarchy, by bringing what's important to the front. And above all, you'll be embracing the Web with a particularly new approach to publishing.

This *is* new thinking for a new medium.

# Afterword

Now that you know the principles of Web design, there's nothing left to do but start screaming. Or, if screaming is not compatible with your psychological makeup, more subtle methods of personal influence can be applied. At HotWired we are partial to sarcasm, sophistry, whining, the invention of elaborate metaphor ("You see, the site is like a bag of Doritos, and you're asking people to open it in the middle"), and, when all else fails, French-accented discourses on the nature of the zeitgeist and its relation to the placement of buttons, menus, and links.

In the early days of Web design, the most common admonition delivered to HotWired designers was "You can't do that" – wrap text around images, for instance. Today, in the era of push, Java, JavaScript, and dynamic HTML, that admonition has been replaced with "You can do that, but nobody will understand it." Web design has increasingly come to resemble software design in its complexity and is more like print or even television in its graphical capabilities.

These advances leave Web builders with many options, while subjecting them to unwelcome functional discipline. And since Web interfaces are interactive, mistakes of interpretation become dead ends for users, and failures to communicate show up with depressing clarity in your comprehensive (if not totalitarian) user logs. To make matters worse, users are mentally saddled with traditions of software interface (overlapping windows, 3-D buttons, pulldown menus), which are amazingly rigid despite being almost brand-new. Web interface, it seems, has been arrested in its infancy. Although there are hundreds of remarkable Web sites, even relatively small interface innovations are often baffling to users who are habituated to standard Internet styles and who are commanded at site after site to "click here."

The conflict between our interest in graphical ideas and the powerful clichés of software interfaces means that Web design at HotWired is a constant argument. This argument has no strict sides. Sometimes a designer who just yesterday insisted that using shaded buttons to signal a "hot" area was an unnecessary concession to obviousness will exhaustedly conclude today that the only thing users are likely to understand is a nested list of directories. To which the usually too rational interface experts will giddily reply, "Be brave." More often, of course, the situation is reversed, and I have heard and been party to many hours of spiraling debate among editors, designers, and members of HotWired's interface group, as Jeffrey or one of his colleagues generously attempted to avoid pointing out our craziness while defending the interests of the innocent and not-so-innocent Internet user.

*HotWired Style* captures the stability of our site's design principles but barely suggests the chaos of the development process. No exploration of Web interface can be fruitful without some partner to the dialogue – whether colleague or client – asking questions, disagreeing, or, as we do once in a while, pretending to agree while energetically exploring every forbidden option. If you follow the rules this book offers, you'll have an indispensable foundation for Web site building. But the final principle for successful, if painful, collaboration – disobedience – is the one we leave to you.

Gary Wolf
Executive Producer, HotWired

# Index

innovations in, in response to new media, 136\-37
separating form and function in, 3\-4
Pyramidal website design, 70\-75

**Q**

QuickTime video plug-in, 125, 127, 128

**R**

Readers. *See* Audience, website
Real Audio, Progressive Network, 125, 126
Red Meat <www.redmeat.com>, design for clarity in, 86\-87
Redundancy, building layered pages using, 49\-50
Rough Guide travel-book series online, 36\-39

**S**

Salon <www.salonmag.com>
content changes in, 99\-100
cultural context for design elements in, 54
Save My Settings feature, 142
Screens, creating streams in Web design vs. composing, 89\-93
Scrolling, 92
search.com <www.search.com>, design of, as online library, 12, 13
Search interface, code for HotBot's, 12
Security
code signing for, 133\-34
personal digital certificates for, 145
Self-searching, 12
Server logs, 44
information available from, 143
Server-side image maps, 82
Shockwave, Macromedia, 125
Silicon Graphics, Inc., 59

SimpleText, 31
Simplicity, designing for, 53\-61
color customization and, 56\-57
cultural context and, 54\-55
hyperlinks and, 62\-63
internal virtual context and, 55\-57
Macintosh Human Interface Guidelines and, 60
metaphors and, 58\-61
Single Pixel GIF, iii, 49
*Slate* <www.slate.com>, 137
SoftQuad's HoTMetal Pro, 31(2x's)
Soundtracks, 132
Southwest Airlines <www.iflyswa.com>, use of metaphor in design of, 58\-59
Speed, designing for, 65\-77
bandwidth, connection modes, and, 65, 66
big colors and, 67, 68
grouping images and reducing number of graphic files and, 67\-70
image compression schemes and, 67\-68
Lego toy constructions as analogy and, 76\-77
optimization and, 72
pyramidal structure of websites and, 70\-75
Splashes, 23, 102\-5
daily, 98
Squier, Joseph, 92
Streaming Web pages, vs. composing screens, 89\-93
Style sheets, 34\-35
cascading, 18, 35, 124
W3C on, 72
Suck <www.suck.com>
rule breaking by, 118
subversion of hierarchical design on, 95\-96
Sun's Java language.
*See* Java <www.javesoft.com> programming language; JavaScript

**T**

T1 connections, 66
Tables, laying out Web pages using, 32\-33
Talk.com, HotWired, 148
Teasers
animated (splashes), 23
customized, 118
rotating, 18\-20
Television, 108, 142
degradability of, 42
speed of message delivery in, 65
Templates, daily content changes using, 99
Text
coupling of, with icons, 83
graphics off setting for displaying only, 47
placement of links in, 116
Threads system, HotWired, 148
Time, divisions of content based on, 97\-98
Tracking, Web audience, 143\-46

**U**

URLs
displaying of destination, 82
replacing with descriptive pointers, 117
unique-session IDs in, 145
Usage patterns of Web, 66
tracking, 142\-43, 145
Users. *See* Audience, website

**V**

Validation of HTML code, 30
Video in websites, 125, 127, 128
first frame of, 125
Virtual context for design elements, 55\-57
Virtual reality modeling language (VRML) <www.vrml.org/>, 59\-60
Visual consistency, 56

# Colophon

This is the first Wired book to print directly from computer to plate using PostScript® technology by Quad/Graphics, Inc.

Composed pages were converted to PostScript through a PS2 system and translated into Scitex language using software version 4.12. RIP'd files were then sent to Scitex Prisma workstations. Final graphic images and text were electronically imposed using a Creo Thermal Platesetter 3244. The book was printed on a Heidelberg Harris M1000B web press and bound on a Sheridan UB545 binder.

Hardware used to design this book included Apple Power Macintosh and Power Computing computers, Radius Precision Color Displays, Sony monitors, Hewlett-Packard LaserJet 5si, and a Xerox Majestic 5790 digital color copier. Software included QuarkXpress, Adobe PhotoShop and Illustrator.

The text is set in Adobe Myriad, a 2-axis multiple master font designed by Carol Twombly and Robert Slimbach. FontShop's FFThesis Mono designed by Lu(ca)s de Groot was used for all technical code and FontBank, Inc.'s Addled was used for all headlines.

Cover Design and Creative Direction by Barbara Kuhr. Art Direction and design by Susanna Dulkinys. Design and layout by Juliette Robbins for Danielseed Design. Production Art Direction by Eugene Mosier. Other indespensible hands included Sean Cullen, Matthew McCarthy, and Katja Grubitzsch.